Carry Me

Carry Me

Christine Wyrtzen's Discoveries on the Journey into God's Arms

as told to
Jerry B. Jenkins

MOODY PRESS
CHICAGO

ISBN: 0-8024-2836-3

1 2 3 4 5 6 Printing/BC/Year 92 91 90 89 88

Printed in the United States of America

Dedication

The story of my journey is dedicated to those who renew my spirit. To those in whom I have witnessed God's miracle of grace. To those who became His hands when I needed to know God was very much alive and approachable. The thought of each of you makes my heart smile.

God has not been trying out an experiment on my faith to test its quality. He knew it already. It was I who didn't.

C. S. Lewis

Acknowledgments

It is rarely easy to place your thoughts and feelings on paper. Each chapter of this book has provided a new challenge, a new adventure, and I cannot put a value on the support that I have consistently received from you, my friends, during this process. Your belief level in this project has been unwavering since the introduction of the idea six years ago.

Jerry, do you remember the first time you suggested the idea of a book honoring my mother? Little did we know that your suggestion would result in a collaboration of energy and effort—and the friendship that has been born. I will cherish the memory of the three days we spent sitting in my living room, sharing tears and laughter. Thank you for your commitment to me and to this book.

The staff at Moody Press is to be applauded, especially Greg Thornton and Dana Gould. Patience is a virtue, and you have certainly exemplified that strength as you allowed us the time we needed to work and rework the story that these pages contain. You have made it possible for us to develop a statement in which we firmly believe.

And the deadline would not have been met without the teamwork of those I love. Thank you to our staff—Paula, Shawna, Jean, and Ruth Ann for your all-night editing events. Julie, Ann, Debbie, Betty, Donna, Jeanette, Ruby, and Lynne—thank you for reading and evaluating over these many months. And Larry, your hours at the computer saved all of us a significant amount of time and energy. The candid and constructive feedback that all of you have offered has taught me much about myself. Your gifts, offered to this project and to our ministry on a daily basis, are vital as we offer "encouragement for successful living."

Nancy, you have been the mirror into which I have reflected many ideas. You have willingly set aside your own dreams to see this book born. I value your heart and look forward to the relationship we will enjoy for the rest of our lives. Mom must be smiling at the bond growing between us.

Paula, words cannot express my commitment to you and my appreciation of the investment you have made in my life. You are the author waiting to find time to write. Many times your own goals have been postponed because of your desire to help others reach theirs. You are my friend—constant and encouraging through the many challenges of rebirth.

And finally, Ron, Jaime, and Ryan, no longer will the sound of my constant typing permeate our home—at least not for a while. You have been patient when dinner was an hour late and graciously submitted to fast-food outings! My love for you, Ron, continues to grow. You have supported me in this endeavor as strongly as you have in my singing ministry. Thank you for believing in me when I have sometimes ceased to believe in myself.

My friends, I have been made all the richer because I am walking beside you. And now, united, we extend our hands to encourage others along their journey into God's arms.

Introduction

I will always be filled with wonder when I see God touch someone deeply and profoundly through music. At home, in a lower desk drawer, rest a dozen letters that I take out often and reread when I'm in need of encouragement. Most tell how a particular song has made a difference in the way the writer has handled life. There is no greater joy than to know that because you communicate truth through music, people's lives are changed, sometimes dramatically.

For Those Who Hurt, an album designed especially for those struggling with life, was born as a result of the song "The Fire." Although it had been placed in the middle of one of my albums, and every song around it varied thematically, God still dramatically used the song to penetrate layers of personality and bring comfort to the deepest part of the human soul. Seeing how God had used this one song made me wonder how much more He could use a whole album structured around encouragement.

For Those Who Hurt became more than an album that changes audiences. It changed me. With its release dawned a growing awareness of the devastation that has been wrought in our imperfect world. The content of the mail we received began to change significantly. Instead of a one-page letter inquiring about the printed music of a favorite song, eight- to ten-page letters came from anguished souls asking for help. At times I felt too young and inexperienced to handle such heavy-duty questions.

Seeking to communicate the *For Those Who Hurt* material, I began to restructure my concerts to touch the hurting person. Most of the second half became a platform for addressing issues such as handicaps, illness, and the pain of rejection and divorce.

One month after the album's release, I was confronted with an application of its truth. God in His sovereignty knew ahead of time that I should speak from my experience. Through personal loss He was giving me the opportunity to internalize the message I had begun to share with people. Thus far, it had been told from a painless platform of inexperience.

Four years have gone by since the initial request was made to write this book. I have tried twice to accomplish this during these years, only to stop and realize that my heart had not yet learned enough. I do not profess to be an authority on the subjects addressed between these two covers. Many fine books have been written from doctrinal and clinical viewpoints. My intent is to share personal struggles, failures, and victories through which you might gain added insight, to give practical tools as you look for creative ways to extend God's comfort to others, and even more important, to offer encouragement should you feel alienated from God and His people. Whoever you are and whatever your situation, I care. The Lord Jesus understands. And God the Father loves you deeply.

The Music Called "Life"

A musical masterpiece contains both peaks and valleys. A climax will be more fully appreciated after experiencing tension and dissonance. So it is with life. Those who know real joy are those who have suffered profound sadness. Only those who have peeked through death's door can know the true exhilaration of living.

1

Thanksgiving Day started out like all the others. Nothing hinted that this day would reveal the first crack in an otherwise idyllic life. While the sixteen-pound turkey started to brown and sizzle in the oven and I began to put together the crust for apple dumplings, I experienced no premonition that this day would mark the beginning of a journey into foreign territory.

The aroma of turkey began to permeate our home. Jaime perched herself on the island in the kitchen and watched me wrap the cored apples in crust and get them ready to go in the oven. Ron had offered to vacuum the house, and I had set the dining room table the night before. Everything was running on schedule, and I expected my parents and sister Nancy to arrive by noon. They would be making a two-hour trip to reach our home in upstate New York.

About the time I expected to hear their car pull in the driveway, the phone rang. It was Nancy.

"We're going to be late," she said. "Mom wasn't feeling well this morning. I took her blood pressure and got an unusual reading. She's been resting and says she feels up to coming now. We'll be there in two hours."

I hung up the phone, turned down the temperature on the turkey, and poured Ron and myself a cup of coffee. We talked about the possible implications of Nancy's call. But not being accustomed to unsettling news, we dismissed the idea of it being anything serious on the grounds that after a short rest she was already feeling better.

They arrived two hours later. Mom took her time coming up the stairs from the garage where their car was parked. She did look a bit pale, I had to admit. However, as was her style, she quickly shifted the attention away from herself. She admired the way the table was set and then played all kinds of guessing games as to what was cooking and filling the kitchen with delicious smells. The meal went smoothly, and because we were together, the enjoyment level was high. Holidays were always fun. A time to sit by candlelight, have unlimited refills of coffee, and reminisce of holidays past.

Before preparing to make the trip back home, the subject did turn to her bad spell that morning. It was agreed that upon returning home, she would visit the family doctor and have some blood work done to determine the cause of the blood pressure readings.

Actually there had been some warning signs in previous weeks that something was wrong. Mom and Dad had taken a trip to Germany in October. Foreign travel had been a lifelong dream, and they had saved for years to take this vacation. Dad wanted to visit the places where he had been stationed while fighting in World War II. Mom was a European history lover. Her time as a librarian in our small town gave her hundreds of hours to become an expert on Nazi Germany. In fact, she had even corresponded with an imprisoned German officer after reading his autobiography. She had been anxious to go but had experienced signs of ill health throughout their travels.

After Thanksgiving we all resumed our daily routines. I anticipated the release of the album we had finished earlier that year—*For Those Who Hurt.* I was both excited and apprehensive because the album was unique. It was music designed for hurting people, and there was nothing like it in the marketplace. As with any pioneering effort, it ran the risk of failure.

One morning in late November I received a call from Paula, my partner in the ministry. She told me that the album was to be shipped to bookstores that day. We discussed the opposition we had seen as we had tried to get the album from the creative stage to the point of completion. Half-seriously she said, "Well, I wonder what's going to happen to us today?" suggesting that Satan might launch one of his greatest attacks on the actual day of the album's release.

The rest of the afternoon was uneventful. Just before midnight, however, the phone woke Ron and me. Paula, her husband, Larry, and their two children had been in a serious car accident. Larry's condition was critical. Paula had a serious concussion. Their five-year-old daughter was in the hospital with a broken pelvis. I immediately made plans to fly to Cincinnati.

This was my first close encounter with tragedy. My exterior appeared calm and self-assured as I arrived at the hospital to see Larry. At this point, he had not seen his wife or children, since they were also seriously injured. I inquired at the front desk as to the location of his room and took the elevator to the second floor. I walked down the corridor of intensive care, only daring to snatch quick glimpses into the rooms that I passed. Most people inside appeared to barely be hanging onto life. The apparatus surrounding their beds instantly gave me an apprehensive feeling. I renewed my commitment to maintain my composure and appear strong.

I reached Larry's room, peeked around the corner, and thought I had made a mistake. I hardly recognized the person who lay in the bed. The six-foot, two-hundred-pound man I knew now looked ghastly, his usual healthy color was chalky gray. His face was drawn and his cheeks sunken. I saw him open his eyes and look at me. I immediately went to his side and assured him that the rest of his family was all right. Unable to talk because of the tubes in his throat, he listened intently and then started to cry. I cradled his head in my arms and cried along with him.

Exhausted, I left five minutes later. This new world I was entering seemed so foreign. I had trouble verbalizing, even to myself, how deeply all this was affecting me and what my reactions really were. The time to probe my feelings was cut short because I had to return to Paula. She and the rest of her family desperately needed my help.

Two nights later Larry developed a blood clot in his lung, and his doctor called to tell us that he might not make it through the night. Paula and I sat up most of the night praying that God would intervene and that Larry would somehow survive. Miraculously, he pulled through. My first exposure to tragedy ended by God answering my prayers exactly as I had prayed. Of course, we know that it is not always a part of God's plan to answer our petitions in the way we ask Him, but thankfully my introduction to this kind of trauma ended as I hoped.

Meanwhile Mom kept her appointment with the doctor, who prescribed a complete blood work-up. The results indicated that her hemoglobin level was dangerously low. She had lost a lot of blood and was severely anemic. She was put in the hospital for immediate transfusions and further tests to ascertain the point of blood loss.

Even after hearing this, I was still convinced that there was nothing seriously wrong. How could someone who had walked around Munich a few weeks earlier be seriously ill? I called Nancy often from Paula's house to find out the results of the tests. So far the doctors had found nothing to alarm them, and they were beginning to show optimism. My mom was in good spirits, making conversation with nurses on duty, telling jokes to the orderlies, and amusing the housekeeping staff by stripping her own bed and delivering her dirty laundry to them. They all agreed she was one of a kind.

Finally, after being sure that Larry was healing well, I scheduled a flight home. The night before I was to leave, I called Nancy to see if the doctors had reached any conclusions.

"Christine" she said slowly, "when will you be home?"

"Tomorrow," I said. She thought for a moment and continued, "Why don't you call me when you get back, and we'll talk about it."

I probed no further, but inside a part of me died. I cried most of the night. I didn't want to trouble Paula; after all, she was trying to recover from her own crisis. But intuitively she knew something was wrong.

"It's my mom," I said. "I just know something's drastically wrong."

"You don't know that, Chris," she said trying to encourage me. "Maybe you're just reading into it."

"No, I know. Something's really wrong."

I was to change planes in Pittsburgh, and I was frustrated throughout the whole flight. I couldn't stand the tension, not knowing for sure. I had to find out. As soon as we landed in Pittsburgh, I hurried off the plane and found a phone booth.

"Nancy, it's me," I said softly.

"Are you home?"

"No, but I really want to know."

"Are you sure?"

"Yes."

"Well, it's not good."

Time stood still. I had known it was bad news from the moment Nancy had delayed giving me answers the night before. A barrier, a defense mechanism rose up in me to fend off the news, but it had failed. I couldn't wait. I had to know. I had to call from Pittsburgh. And so there I was. Alone. In a phone booth. Between flights. When she asked me if I were sure I wanted to know, the very last vestige of optimism vanished. Nancy had been calm and objective, no doubt to protect me. I could say nothing. She continued.

"They found a tumor. They can't operate because it's vascular." Nancy was a medical student. She understood that. The tumor had vessels, ducts, and it carried blood. To

19

operate would be to threaten a major blood supply. I didn't know anything of tumors, of blood supplies, of medicine. I only knew that I was right; my worst fears were confirmed. How could this be happening? I was nearly thirty years old and still called her mommy. And now my big sister was telling me what? That Mommy had a tumor? Cancer? Inoperable?

My head was light. My ears rang. It was as though I were on some strong medication that left me numb. I was aware of my isolation, how ominous this moment was in my life. "Nancy, have they said how much time she has?"

The slight pause told all. "Well, it could be as little as three months."

I remember nothing more of the conversation. I know we talked further about Mom, but it was not registering with me. Finally it occurred to me to ask, "How are you taking it?"

"OK," she said. But I could tell Nancy was thinking of me, of the last leg of my flight to Albany and then the two-hour drive north to Schroon Lake. "Would you like for someone to come to Albany to meet you?"

"No. I'll be all right." But I wasn't. If she hadn't known it before, she knew it when I told her that I loved her. Sadly, we were not in the habit of making such expressions to each other. We thought it was cool to greet after long absences by just shaking pinkies. The problem was, it *was* cool. Too cool.

If my gate had not been a few steps from that phone booth, I doubt that I would have been able to find it. My travels frequently take me through Pittsburgh, and I can never pass that phone booth without recalling the conversation that forever changed my life.

I was to learn some life-changing lessons over the next several years. They would not be easy, but growth never is. If something I have learned can make your journey easier, then this book will have been worth the effort. As I like to say in my concerts, I wish I could share an ex-

20

tended cup of coffee with you, listen to you, and really get to know you. What joy it would bring to be able to share with you some of what God has taught me.

And what was my time in the valley to reveal? That my view of God was too small. This was evidenced with the passing of time. "Mom has cancer" were simple words, yet the ramifications were so far reaching that my beliefs crumbled, being reduced to nothing but questions.

I share my story with you because I care. You will not be given a series of platitudes or a list of verses to memorize. There are no quick fixes to alleviate the havoc that our imperfect world deals us. Our emotional responses are complex. However, God's arms are strong enough to carry us through the deepest waters.

Creating the Hook

Songs. Words with music. The development of a musical expression that will reach people at the deepest center of the soul requires a vision of the end product and an unwavering determination to see the process through. But when that venture to reach the soul is successfully completed, the efforts extended are well rewarded.

And how is the journey begun? One must first have a message or "hook." The hook is a well-stated purpose wrapped in a fresh choice of words. As no two snowflakes are alike, no two songs and no two lives exactly parallel. Each person is unique, having been formed by a background of experiences different from all others.

The heart of the child produces the personality, the behavior, the unique, individual "hook" of the adult he is to become.

2

Perhaps the greatest good that suffering can work for a believer is to increase the capacity of his soul for God. The greater our need, the greater will be our capacity; the greater our capacity, the greater will be our experience of God. Can any price be too much for such eternal good?

Margaret Clarkson

I had been keeping a journal for years; jotting down a few entries now and then. I had made only two in the year leading up to that night in Pittsburgh. But after a numbing flight and drive, and a sensitive reception from Ron, I made my last journal entry. I titled it "Day of the News," dated December 13, 1982.

> I have just called home and heard from Nancy. Mommy has cancer. Inoperable. Spreading fast. She has only a few months.
>
> I am unemotional, calm. How can that be? I guess my mind simply rejects such information. I cannot make myself believe it, however hard I try.
>
> Oh, my dear Mommy. The thought of her not being here is inconceivable. I cannot survive this. I must be dreaming.
>
> God, how can You do this to my mother? How can You take her when I still call her "Mommy"?

A lyricist has to have a bit of a poet in her, but when I reviewed this journal entry the next day, I saw no poetry, no pretty words. It was raw, stark. I was beyond describing how I felt. Even after insisting that I was unemotional and calm, I sobbed uncontrollably. I never wrote in my journal again. It was too painful. Although subsequent entries probably would have been valuable pieces of personal history, my heart was too fragile to see the facts in print.

Now, through impending personal tragedy and loss, I had to internalize the message I had recently been led to share through *For Those Who Hurt*. I was to learn what vulnerability was all about. I would no longer be ministering from an objective platform, handing out doses of spiritual truth like medicine to those wrestling with life. I was now frail. Only a most powerful God could work through such a weak vessel, one whose mother was dying.

The thought that my mother was terminally ill was beyond my comprehension. The fact that I couldn't deal with reality was a clue to the intricate defense mechanism that I had developed against unpleasant truth. It was a complex escape I had contrived over the years without realizing it.

The cold truth was to hit me between the eyes. When it did, I felt helpless. I had been thrust onto a course I was convinced I could not travel, yet there was no choice. Could I hide behind pat answers? Would the self-protective shock that kept me artificially calm carry me over the deepest ruts in the road ahead? Or was it merely another self-protective response?

I had never considered for more than a moment the death of either of my parents—probably because I believed I couldn't survive it. I didn't deliberately avoid such thoughts, but subconscious fears often block reality. Did I believe our family was immune to death? Not consciously, certainly. Everyone dies. How naive to consider birth and growing older a part of life, yet not death.

When I was able to temporarily force shut the door of denial, keeping reality from penetrating my world, I tried to put back in place my calm exterior and resume the routine of life. But nothing was the same. Nothing had meaning. I felt numb, removed from my feelings, removed from life itself, removed from God. The cracks in my faith, as revealed in my journal entry, were signs of erosion that eventually challenged my theology to its roots. I asked God why and received no answer. Was He silent, or could I simply not hear Him? Spiritually I felt alone. I lived with a stranger, and the stranger was me. I asked questions as basic as, Can I trust God? only to realize that if I couldn't or wouldn't trust Him, I could depend on no one else.

Reality was forcing open the door of denial, and I didn't like it. As much as I leaned and pushed and kicked to keep the door shut, it kept opening. Reality came in the form of full-colored memories, ones that transported me back to a childhood that I feared would be lost with my mother's death. Dozens of images, alive with sounds and smells, appeared in snatches. I daydreamed of bacon and onion frying in a pan, Mom's graceful demonstrations on the ice while teaching Nancy and me figure eights, coming home from school to the sweet smell of homemade bread, and going into Mom's bedroom late at night to find her reading.

These were things I was not ready or willing to lose. With this persistent truth came tears, weeping that worked its way up from the core of my being with a grief so profound that I couldn't contain it. How could I begin to prepare for a life without her, without the treasured memories that had always been a part of my childhood home?

*   *   *

Petersburg, New York, sits in a valley on the borders of Vermont and Massachusetts. In that Norman Rockwell setting, Nancy and I were raised in a one-hundred-year-old, three-story Victorian house that sat high on a hill overlooking the river. Dad was a science and math teacher in our local school system, a supervising principal, and later served as a guidance counselor for the remainder of his working years. It is difficult to assess in which position he most excelled. During his tenure as principal, his friendly easygoing way was balanced with a high regard for law and order. For instance, if a high-school boy was caught smoking, Dad might keep him after school and require that he dig a six-foot by three-foot "grave" to bury the remains of the cigarette. His creativity is still the talk of many local residents. Many of his former students, now in their forties, attribute much of their present success to his approach toward education. His personal discipline and strength of character is evidenced in his teaching of a Sunday school class for forty years, consistent 5:30 A.M. devotions, and an unwavering resolve to daily live his convictions.

Mom was a homemaker. And what a home she made! She was the most efficient of managers. Routine was established, and rarely did we deviate from it. We were never left with baby-sitters. Dad never traveled away from home. I was a teenager the first time he was gone for a weekend. Everything at the Hewitt household revolved around the family. We may have been a reflection of the TV series "Father Knows Best." We wouldn't have known, for we didn't have a television until I was a teenager, but we rarely missed it. Nancy and I lived full lives. We both were immersed in music, starting piano lessons at age four. We rode bikes, climbed trees, built forts in the woods, ice skated in the winter, and were avid swimmers. There was also the Petersburg Baptist Church where Mom and Dad held numerous positions. We were front and center at every meeting, and those activities filled the remainder of our spare time.

We were not affluent, living on a school teacher's salary, neither did we consider ourselves deprived. We thought nothing of venturing into a swanky section of a nearby Massachusetts town for a secondhand coat. When I see and hear kids today (yes, my own included) asking for things they see in a store, I wish I knew how my parents prevented us from begging. Eating out was a luxury, too.

In the early years, I recall dining at a nice restaurant maybe once a year.

My mother was an important key to the closeness in our family. She had a quality that made everyone want to be involved in whatever she was doing. She was magnetic. Even when I was five years old, I can remember following her around, asking to take part in adult activities so I could be near her.

She had extraordinary dignity and grace that gave one the impression that she was comfortable interacting with any group of people. Extremely well-read, Mom could offer an answer to nearly any question. She could just as easily give a gardening tip, a World War II fact, or advise on the best kind of wood to burn for winter's fuel.

There was an eccentric part of her, however, that gave her such an interesting flair that people found it difficult to categorize her personality. She was industrious. She would rise early in the morning, take meticulous care of the birds, and then stride cheerfully into the kitchen, saying, "What a beautiful morning! Let's see. What shall we do today?" She had so much initiative that the rest of us groaned. Mom had a great love for blueberry picking, but she was never satisfied to pick at a commercial farm. She preferred the adventure of hunting for wild berries and usually kept the location of her best bushes a secret. We teased her unmercifully, for she seemed oblivious to such nuisances such as mosquitoes, thornbushes, and rain. The teasing was ignored, and she continued picking berries, aware only of the joy in filling her quart containers. We called her fingers blueberry rakes. No one picked faster. Dad, out of sheer necessity, would go outfitted with mosquito netting over his head. They were quite a sight going off into the woods.

Once the blueberries were home, they usually found their way into muffins, which earned a reputation for being the best in the valley. The remaining berries were used in her buttermilk pancakes, and the thought of them makes my mouth water even now. Everyone teased her about baking for half the town. She was known for her generosity with the neighbors. It wasn't just something she did to receive praise or attention. She really cared. She was the one who was often there during the difficult times, who sat with the elderly on their deathbeds when they had no other family to care. The family joke was that our house was a refuge for troubled souls—widows, distraught spouses, those contemplating suicide. Many ended up on our doorstep.

Saturday was usually spent getting ready for Sunday. Bible school lessons were prepared, and since Nancy and I held the organist and pianist positions from the age of ten, we spent some of the day picking out preludes and offertories.

Mom cooked all day Saturday preparing for our Sunday meal after church. It was always the feast of the week and was the time we did most of our entertaining. I cannot begin to count the number of guest speakers, missionaries, and singles who sat around the table after church, enjoying quality conversation and a superb meal.

My teenage years were not difficult. I did not experience the need to question my parents' values or establish my own independence. Much of the reason for this, I'm sure, was the level of my involvement at Word of Life. I began playing for crusades and summer camps by the time I was twelve and spent most weekends, holidays, and summers in ministry there. Without complaint, my parents drove me all over the East Coast to Word of Life rallies so I could continue to enjoy an outlet for my music. It was at Word of Life Ranch that I met my future husband, Ron. He is the son of Jack Wyrtzen, founder of the ministry. We became good friends and dated all through high school and college.

We married in the spring of 1973 and moved to Texas so he could continue his aviation training at LeTourneau College. Following this, we returned to Word of Life where we directed the junior high camp and where Ron did some flying. We were to stay in that ministry for twelve years.

We settled in, without much adjustment at all, to happily married life. We have rarely known discord. We seem to enjoy the same perceptions about matters both important and trivial. We share a common taste in everything from food to clothes to colors for our home. Over the years we would cultivate and enjoy the friendship of our relationship. We find it easy to tackle projects together, whether it's working out in the yard or wallpapering a bathroom.

It appeared to most that Pollyanna had married Prince Charming and that they would live happily ever after. Actually, that was pretty accurate until a couple of years into our marriage, when our marriage hit its first snag.

Writing the Melody

The melody. The sounds that enhance the lyrics we wish to communicate. It is foundational to the success of any song. When creating it, one needs to keep in mind the final intention—the marriage of lyrics and music. Likewise, our life's partners—those parents, siblings, mates, and children that accompany us—play a profound part in the song each life can sing.

3

I have always loved babies. When I was ten, our family took care of a four-month-old baby for several weeks. She was a product of a neglected, underprivileged home. Penny became a member of our family. It was a highlight of my childhood. Like most little girls, I lived in a fantasy world where my plastic dolls became real. This kind of imaginary play was the best way I had found to satisfy my strong desire to mother.

In our third year of marriage, Ron and I suspected we might have difficulty conceiving children. Tests by our doctor revealed that I was an unlikely candidate for pregnancy.

The inability to conceive is a terrible blow to most women. I quickly learned the sense of grief that overcomes a woman who desperately wants and needs to be a mother but cannot conceive. Infertility became the first blemish on my neat and tidy life.

Determined to be parents, we did not mourn our loss —our ability to conceive—for long. Perhaps in this way we were not typical. Whether we had biological children or were blessed through adoption made little difference. I was to come in contact with many couples who struggle with infertility. My acceptance of our need to adopt did not leave me unsympathetic, however, to those who feel a strong sense of loss at not being able to bear their own children. Few understand the ordeal, including the barren woman herself. It is real and difficult, and the number of women who suffer is staggering.

I began seeing numerous cases where adoption had assuaged the grief over barrenness. So as soon as Ron and I knew why our efforts to have our own child had failed, we looked into adopting. There were those who advised me to have surgery to correct the blockage, but down deep I wasn't comfortable with that. If I could have submitted to such a procedure without feeling as if I would be violated as a person, I might have decided differently. Every woman has her own built-in limit related to the intervention of medicine in the treatment of infertility. We should respect ourselves enough to honor our discomfort level. The surgery wasn't for me, and I still feel strongly about the decision I made.

Adoption is not without its own set of frustrations. Some agencies predicted a five-year waiting period. We found one agency, however, that told us we would wait only one year. Once we were screened, had our home study completed, and filled out all the paperwork, I decided that a one-year wait would be just like being pregnant. I redecorated a room in our house for the nursery. I wallpapered it in orange and yellow clowns, refinished Ron's baby crib, washed all the baby clothes I had collected over the years, lined the drawers, and tenderly filled them.

Every time we walked by the freshly decorated room, we experienced a wonderful sense of anticipation. We were certain that any day the phone would ring, and we would hear the news of the birth of our first child.

The days turned into months; three Christmases without a child passed. Four years came and went. How neat and tidy it can all sound. So painless to see in print that four years passed. But quite another thing to have lived it. We had now been married seven years and had long since abandoned subjecting ourselves to the sight of the nursery. The fresh paint gave way to discoloration and the freshly washed clothes turned musty. We turned the heat down in the room and left the door closed for months on end. It was simply too painful to acknowledge. In the meantime my singing ministry began to grow, and although I was enjoying the beginning of something new in the area of music, I also had to deal with those who whispered behind my back that I had abandoned my dreams of motherhood, exchanging them instead for a career. Most did not know that we had been struggling with infertility and had been camping out by the phone for four years waiting for some word about our baby. The accusations stung.

Late one day in June 1979, we were contacted by a pastor whom Ron and I had met on the road. He told us of a teenage girl in his church who was pregnant and due to deliver during the summer. He asked if we were interested in pursuing this option. We responded with a resounding yes. We contacted a lawyer, filled out more paperwork, and prepared to wait.

We were eating supper one night when we were called and informed that the birth mother was in labor. We paced like cats, beside ourselves for the rest of the evening. Just before midnight we learned that we were the parents of a nine-pound, healthy baby girl. The door to the nursery was swung wide open, and the baby clothes washed once again. I went out that next morning and bought birth announcements appropriate for adoption and filled them out. We named our daughter Jaime Susannah.

Although I was yet to see my baby, I am convinced that if I had been required to pick her out of the hospital nursery full of babies, I could have done it. The sense of attachment was that strong.

Three days later we were handed our little girl in the parking lot of our lawyer's office. Ron and I had waited years to experience this moment, which was beyond description. My empty arms were full.

I reveled in motherhood. I had worked with a close friend for several months prior to Jaime's birth, refinishing a cradle that had been in my family for two hundred years. Jaime could now sleep in as perfect a world as I could create for her. Several good friends made baby quilts. Wall hangings and smocked dresses further evidenced that she was wanted and welcomed into our family and our circle of friends. Life seemed almost perfect again, and the shadows of hurt could be forgotten.

Ron and I agreed that I should take Jaime with me for my next year of concerts. Babies travel easily, and in many ways being on the road was such a natural way of life for me that I didn't think twice about taking her. Besides, the travel time gave me many extra hours each day to hold her and strengthen our bond. There were those, however, who began to criticize our decision. That rattled me. I wanted everyone in my life to approve and agree with everything I did. This unrealistic need would surface later with more serious implications, but for now it was simply a nuisance and a symptom of a tendency in my personality that should have been confronted. The pattern would operate unchecked for many more years.

Two years later we began thinking about adopting again. This time we put our names into several agencies. Access to promising sources proved easier this time since I was sharing the story of Jaime's adoption in every concert.

We were contacted the first week in June 1982 by an agency not far from our home. They had a little girl for us. A small baby, only six pounds. We quickly fixed up the guest room and transformed it into a nursery. Out came all of the baby clothes. I had fun looking at everything Jaime had worn, and I tried picturing it again on our new daughter. We named her Julie.

Unless a couple has endured it personally, one cannot know the pain we suffered when the news came that Julie would not be coming to us after all. Her mother had decided to keep her. Once again we were faced with a love for a child we would never see blossom into a relationship. We looked once again at a finished nursery—and we felt as empty as those who give birth to a stillborn child.

This experience was the one that bred the creation of the song "Carry Me." Friends who were able to have their own children couldn't seem to understand the loss. Some even said, "We understand that you are disappointed, but it's not like you knew the baby. You never even saw her." The failure of people to perfectly relate was quickly evident. During times like these, the hurting one is driven to the only One who can walk with us in perfect empathy.

A few weeks later we were contacted by another agency, informing us that we would have our second child soon. It was the following week that our son was born. We named him Ryan Dean, sharing the same middle name with his father.

Now a contented family of four, we settled into life. But the grim reality of living in an imperfect world had to be recognized. I began to notice situations that made Romans 8:28 appear a mockery to me. Situations didn't always seem to work together for good. Events weren't consistently smooth in my life or in the lives of those around me. Subtle signs of decay were penetrating my idyllic perception of life, causing readjustment and redefinition.

The Producer's Role

Early in the writing and recording process competent producers are needed. Their mission is to unite all the components, pulling together talented, expressive people, capable technicians, and adequate facilities to insure the development of the best possible product.

Pain can fragment even the strongest of lives, leaving its victim in scattered pieces. The pulling together of all the segments requires the tenderness of the only One capable of producing eternal joy.

4

One of the first lessons I learned on this journey was how to (and how not to) talk to a hurting person. The day after I heard the shattering news of my mother's cancer, a good friend walked into my kitchen, wrapped her arms around me, and cried. I can't tell you how much that meant to me. Nothing means quite as much to a hurting person as someone who is willing to share a loss. Few are willing to make that kind of emotional investment.

Ironically, my friend felt she had shown weakness, that she had not been strong for me. I wish I could convince her that her willingness to weep with me was as therapeutic as anything anyone else said or did for me during that traumatic time. It was a moment I will never forget. It said more than any words could ever say. The fact that someone is willing to share the hurt may be just the incentive that prevents a person from giving up.

A few days later I was in church, and I admit, merely going through the motions. My emotions had been undressed, and I was aching. My mother's illness was the only thing on my mind, seemingly twenty-four hours a day. As we made our way out after the service, I heard my name from across the parking lot.

I turned to see a respected leader of our church with his hands cupped around his mouth. "Hey, I heard about your mother! How is she?"

What was I supposed to do, yell back across a crowded parking lot, "She's dying! That's how she is!" I'm sure he was trying to express concern, but how I wished he had shown more sensitivity in the way he addressed this painful subject.

I became aware that I was walking a tightrope. I expected more compassion from the family of God, and when they did not deliver I became angry. One of the most difficult parts of the journey was frequently feeling disappointed by people's reactions.

Sometimes God seemed silent, and I slipped easily into despair. Occasionally, though, when I needed it most, someone would reach out to me—someone like the friend who wept with me that first day. During those times I was consoled to my depths and reassured that God was alive and taking care of me.

I was amazed at Ron's sensitivity. I shouldn't have been, because the Lord had given me a husband who was reared by a mother who was in poor health. He understood the pain of watching a loved one's health regress. Ron grew up with many memories of his mother being whisked away by an ambulance. His personal grieving had been a lengthy process that enabled him to identify with the implications that arise with cancer.

A close friend who has lived with a critically ill husband and three small children wrote me a note shortly after she learned of my mother's diagnosis. It's an example of communication that truly helped:

> My dear friend,
>   You have been heavy on my mind and heart today after I heard the news about your mom. I just wanted to write a few thoughts that I pray can be of comfort and encouragement to you. You've "been there" for me time and again over the past few tumultuous years, and I count it a joy to have the privilege of "being there" for you. You are very special and precious to me. I am aware that each of us reacts dif-

ferently to the same situation, and I am by no means trying to minimize your pain by telling you I think I know how you feel. But due to the circumstances I've faced with a person I dearly love, I think I can relate.

There are probably some things you can't openly express, even to yourself, but let me tell you what the Lord laid on my heart concerning you:

I believe with all my heart that the Lord gave you a very special calling to produce the *For Those Who Hurt* album. It has blessed many hurting people—exhorting, encouraging, and even giving opportunity to let the healing tears fall.

I believe also that the Lord has for you now another even higher calling in that He has allowed you this deeply personal trial so you can live out and, yes, be encouraged by the very principles you have so beautifully written, sung, and used to minister to others.

Suffering, and letting God be glorified in it, is a most difficult and most precious calling all wrapped up in one package. Both tears and rejoicing are integral parts. You will experience this in the months ahead.

Please let me know if you ever need to express yourself to someone who's been down the same road . . . whether it's anger (it happens!), hurt, or praise. I go through all of these with the Lord over and over again. If you do express anger to the Lord, He will say, "No wonder," because He'll remember that you're a friend of mine!

How much more meaningful that letter was than the typical comments we often make to each other during times of crisis. "I know what you're going through" (when most often we really don't). "I know how you feel" (when we might not). "It's God's will" (when that's the very truth with which we're struggling).

Mother returned home the day after her diagnosis and began to bake blueberry muffins for some acquaintances on her floor, including some of the doctors and nurses. I knew from that news that she was handling the situation better than I was. She was strong, and I realized that if I choked up, showing my frailty in front of her, I would make her extremely uncomfortable. I would try to be strong around her to keep from creating an awkward situation.

My mother was a smart woman. She knew her death would devastate her loved ones. I put off going to see her for a few days. I wanted some time to picture the scene and muster up enough courage to pull it off. In studying for the *For Those Who Hurt* album, I'd read enough to know the right things to say and do. The question was whether or not I could put myself on automatic pilot.

Until the time of the confrontation, I tried to implement all of the skills I had accumulated while working on the album. I tried to guarantee emotional health by taking heed to those necessary formulas. I constantly preached to myself. *Don't deny your feelings. Think in terms of death. Say it. Death. She's going to die. You don't know when, but she will die. You have to say good-bye in stages and think now what life will be like without her, because if you don't face it now it will be harder later.*

Finally, I was as ready as I would ever be to go home, to face her, to see her. When I walked in I was struck by how normal she looked. I don't know what I had expected —could she already have lost fifty pounds? But there she sat at her desk, answering the mail.

After our greetings, she began, "Look what came today. Have you seen this catalog? How was your trip? How are the kids?"

I replied with the give-and-take of small talk, allowing me to postpone dealing with the big issue. But it was as though we both could read between the lines and hear another conversation, the one down deep, under the protective surface of denial. In my mind I was holding her, crying, as she said, "So, what do you think about me dying of cancer?"

But our thoughts went unspoken. I wanted to say, "I heard, and I know, and I don't like it. I hate it. I'm not ready to give you up, to lose you. Nothing will ever be the same." And I wanted her assurance, and maybe she wanted to say, "Hang in there. We'll get through this together. It's emotionally painful for me, too. How will you handle it? Have you told Jaime?" But those thoughts were never spoken.

It wasn't as if we avoided the issue altogether. It did surface. Mom would say something about whether she would still be around at Christmas, which was just a few days away. Or she would ask me how I liked an outfit, telling me of her intentions to give it to me when it no longer fit her. We talked of doctors, treatments, side effects, and surgery. But we never talked about how we were dealing with these issues of the dying, handling it emotionally.

When I returned to my home to prepare for Christmas, my attitude toward the routine of life was changed. Most of the time I was in a fog. Piercing the mist was a sort of tractor-trailer of reality that instantly brought me to tears. The feeling was so overwhelming and so awful that I had to force myself to move out of its way.

That terrible grief, I learned, would worsen when she actually died. Now I was in the process of picturing all I would miss without her. I began grieving for my children at ages when grandmas are so important to kids.

My parents were coming for ten days over Christmas. I convinced myself that we could rise to this challenge. I welcomed the distraction of having to get ready for it so quickly. My subconscious goal, I realize now, was to persuade myself that everything was perfectly normal and that nothing would change.

Crafting the Lyrics

The lyrics of any song should not be created in haste. Words are the priority. Even the most moving melody line will lose its effectiveness in reaching people if the lyrics are carelessly assembled. Each line, each word, needs to be carefully chosen to accurately reflect the message it intends to convey.

The lyrics of our lives clearly spell out our statement of purpose. What we say through word and action reveals the priorities that motivate and direct us daily. Crafting the message in the light of God's truth, keeping in mind the power of words during the creative process, provides the motivation that propels us toward our ultimate goal: a finished masterpiece.

5

Pain is pain and sorrow is sorrow. It hurts. It limits. It impoverishes. It isolates. It restrains. It works devastation deep within the personality. It circumscribes us in a thousand bitter ways. There is nothing good about it. But the gifts God can give with it are the richest the human spirit can know.

Margaret Clarkson

Several weeks after Christmas I found myself sitting backstage minutes before I had to give a full concert before three thousand college students at a university in Michigan. The objective, confident frame of mind that usually led me onto a concert stage was lost that night in crosscurrents of emotions. I could not get into my usual discipline of spiritually and mentally preparing for a performance. I was caught up in the memories of the Christmas we had just experienced together.

I cling to traditions. I had planned menus that would remind all of us—especially me—that this was like every other holiday. Ron, the kids, and I went to our favorite stores, saw the toy train displays, heard the carolers, and immersed ourselves in our church's Christmas program.

Everyone, including my mother, seemed to enjoy the break. She did all of her usual baking plus more. But a dilemma confronted me. What would we give her for Christmas? What would be practical? And what would depart so much from normalcy that it would scream at us that disease was killing her? That was something we had wanted to forget, just for a while, just for Christmas. We decided on gourmet food, toiletries, lingerie, and an expensive dress. Why the dress? To reaffirm her beauty, to applaud her determination to live life fully to the end. It had been a symbolic message.

And now, somehow, I was expected to do the same—to live life fully. *But how?* I thought. *How can I go out there and give a concert in which the entire second half had been designed to encourage people in pain? My own life was falling apart. How cruel, how unfair. Live life fully? What a sick joke.* I didn't believe I would ever feel like living again.

At that moment I determined that I couldn't face my audience. I wondered if I had enough acting ability to pull it off and appear intact if I changed the songs in the second half.

I rushed to the sound room and frantically chose cassettes that would provide "safe" background music to more comfortable lyrics. That seemed to fix it. After all, who could expect, who would ask me to sing about God's ability to take care of us when my own heart was full of turmoil?

I hardly remember anything about the first half of that concert except that a war was raging inside me. Knowing the second half would contain none of the songs for hurting people, I felt like a hypocrite. I was conveying the image of a woman who had her act together.

Even while I was singing, I asked myself, *Where is true ministry? Where is credibility? Couldn't God be glorified by a voice choked with emotion? Couldn't He be seen in words spoken spontaneously, delivered without eloquence?* I had two options, and the decision I would make would impact everything I did from then on. I could hide in my pain, or I could be vulnerable and honest and bridge that mythical gap between the person on the platform and the audience.

44

I had to be willing to show that I was human and sometimes overwhelmed by life's circumstances. I had to admit to an audience that I was not equipped to handle life and death without the resources of my heavenly Father. I knew I had to face myself and my audience truthfully, regardless of the results or the consequences. I took a deep breath and plunged in.

That night was a milestone in my journey, for it moved me a little further toward genuine transparency between myself and my audience. God, in His tender display of grace, made the second half easier to sing than I had anticipated. That night I made it without stumbling, without crying. Other nights I lost my composure and barely made it through certain songs, but the audiences usually communicated their understanding.

Ironically, I was not as honest with my own family. Few things alienate families faster than enduring difficult times. A husband and wife with an otherwise healthy marriage may lose a child and then find themselves dealing with the loss independently.

As Daddy, Nancy, and I watched my mother's health deteriorate, we were finally able to speak the words *cancer* and *death,* but they were still merely words. They had not yet made their way into the deep areas of the heart where they must eventually be digested as legitimate parts of life.

The three of us talked objectively of the hurt we all experienced but did not allow each other to peek into the corners where panic and helplessness were hidden. We even wept together occasionally, but questions of the soul were asked and dealt with in private. We made our way emotionally alone, struggling to fit our picture of a God of love into our present state of despair.

While making the journey to the bottom of the soul, I had to travel through layers of behavioral patterns, through detours that exposed conflicts between learned theology and my present life. Overall it was rugged introspection. You may be going through that right now, and my hope is that you will find, as I sometimes did, meaningful support for the solitary trek. There is a kind of encouragement from God that builds incentive, that gives us the momentum to stay on course in spite of the pain. Unfortunately, such genuine encouragement from sensitive friends and loved ones is a rare commodity, even within the church —the Body of Christ.

Although I was often bitterly disappointed by other people, I was reminded of the times when I had ducked out the back door after church to avoid having to "think of the right thing to say" to someone who had just lost a loved one. For instance, my stomach knotted when I was approached by someone in a wheelchair after a concert. I was awkward around friends experiencing divorce.

Now I know that any gesture that expresses care is better than sneaking away. Sometimes I still don't know what to say to someone whose mate has been killed in an accident. I can't always offer help in a serious marital battle. But in those situations I always try to show that I care.

At the time I was unaware that my mother was to live longer than the doctors expected. One drug temporarily reduced the size of her tumor, making her feel immeasurably better. But we all, Mom included, knew the truth. These were temporary remissions.

*　　*　　*

During the surprise extension of her life, I was to discover some of the reasons for the church's difficulty in dealing with people in pain. Why is it that the church environment can breed such loneliness, when it is the one place we should consistently find companionship? Many refer to the church as the ultimate caring community, but have you listened to the requests at prayer meetings? People ask for prayer related to job decisions, physical illness, and missionaries. But we rarely hear expressions of discouragement, alcohol and drug dependency, or the hurt caused by the heartbreak of wayward children or mates.

Why?

Too often our churches become exclusive clubs, requiring that if one wishes to be accepted, he assumes their narrow belief system and life-style. It goes far beyond dress codes and standards of conduct. There are definite unwritten laws that prevail. First, one quickly learns there are acceptable and unacceptable sins—ones that may be confessed and others that must be hidden if he is to remain in favorable standing.

The second unwritten commandment is that it is OK to be discouraged or angry, but only for a length of time specified by the track records of the super-spiritual members in the group. If one can ever admit to depression, it should be done only after the fact, when complete victory can be announced.

Being careful not to paint with too broad a brush, the sad fact is that this kind of legalism does not look favorably upon or deal effectively with prolonged struggles. Deep valleys bring periods of doubt and re-evaluation of all that we believe. It can be a traumatic pilgrimage, especially if it's a first crisis. The one making the journey will endure many dark days before realizing that his soul is frail and empty and in need of a loving God. God alone knows how long that takes for each individual.

Too often this process involves lots of questions with seemingly no answers. The legalistics and dogmatists, when they become aware of another's struggle, offer the searching one heavy admonitions. They become Bible-quoting robots, often administering guilt trips that add to the existing questions and doubts. "Therapeutic verses," in the hands of the insensitive legalist, serve as pseudo-spiritual bandages that can cover pain and postpone the work of spiritual healing.

I was fortunate enough to have a small circle of friends who knew how to handle my questions, and when appropriate, help me find answers. Paula, my precious friend who works alongside me in the ministry, willingly admitted that she felt inadequate to know how to support me. She often asked what it was I needed from her. Though sometimes I didn't know how to respond, she did her best to emotionally walk beside me. Her concern was consistent. "I don't know what to say anymore," she would offer, "but I will do anything possible to reach you, to be with you."

I wish I could introduce you to Paula and to all the wonderful people in our ministry who had the near-impossible task of keeping things going at the time when I felt life had stopped. They gently introduced and re-introduced me to the truth that life goes on. They kept concerts, interviews, and deadlines to a minimum. They sent countless personal notes that enriched many difficult days.

They continued to forward letters to me from the office that reminded me that the new album was having an incredible impact. I was still finding it difficult to talk about my mother in my concerts. I hated dealing with pride each time I had to admit that I was not handling it the way the audience might expect, but I became convinced that people should hear from a real person. The responses of sensitive individuals after concerts were confirming my convictions in this matter.

One Friday evening after a concert in Chicago, a woman approached me. She stood out from the others who brought me their albums to autograph or their adopted babies to meet. This simply dressed woman waited her turn and handed me a thick envelope, then walked away without uttering a word.

Intrigued, I took the letter with me, waiting for a quiet moment of solitude when I could read it. That opportunity finally came twenty minutes before the next night's concert. I settled down backstage on some old, canvas-covered boxes. When I opened the letter, I discovered gold.

The woman wrote that she had just said good-bye to her four-year-old son who had died of leukemia. *For Those*

Who Hurt had been of substantial help to her. She also wrote of things she presumed I was dealing with. Her words were so refreshing, so uplifting at a time when my heart was thirsty for a meaningful word. I read her letter nearly every day for a month.

Designing the Arrangement

The arrangement for a song is created to enhance its message. The choice of the sounds of the instruments and the intensity with which they are told to play all affect the singer's ability to communicate the content. And so it is with our faith.

The external evidences reveal much about the vital interaction that takes place in our relationship with the living God. As the melody of life's experiences plays out, it is that time in the valley of suffering that allows others to see past the form of our religion into the heartbeat of a satisfying, fulfilling relationship. And that core reaction to pain will either enhance or detract from the message our lives are asked to sing.

6

Mom and Dad traveled to Boston to seek a second opinion on the treatment of her cancer. After hearing of the great risks of removing a tumor that was largely vascular, Mom decided to forego surgery, wanting to enjoy as many good days as possible. Surgical risks would threaten her chances to do that. While she was trying to enjoy normal days, I found myself detoured into a spiritual wilderness from which I could find no escape. My faith was taking a beating while Mother was sending notes like this to interested friends and relatives in February of 1983:

> After hearing from all the doctors who have been involved with my case, I have decided for the present to forego an operation and will take each day as it comes. With the help of our family physician and local doctors, I will deal with problems as they arise.
>
> I am presently taking Megace, which is a hormone, and according to the oncologist, is in some instances used successfully to retard the growth and spread of the tumor. I am aware that occasionally cancer patients miraculously get well. Of course I would be happy if the Lord chose to perform such a miracle in my case.
>
> I am feeling fairly well these days. I tire more easily but have many opportunities here at home to

rest as needed. Aside from this, my routine is pretty much unchanged.

Love and best wishes,
Gertrude

On Mother's Day it was difficult to tell from her correspondence that she was even sick. Ironically, on that day when my thoughts would normally turn to her, she was thinking of me. Her note, with a bouquet:

Happy Mother's Day to a wonderful daughter—and mother. I thought this floral arrangement looked like one you could create, Chris. We know that you will have a nice day with your family. We love you!

Mother and Dad

But there weren't many "nice" days. I had nightmares so realistic that when I awoke, it took several minutes before I could be sure they had been dreams. I had never been plagued with nightmares before, but now they came every night for a week or two at a time. I would see my mother, looking terrible, on her deathbed in the hospital. The elements were so real that I could smell the alcohol, see the nurses, touch the bedpans, and feel the tubes running in and out of her. I was helpless to do anything to protect her dignity.

Frustration. She is in a coma. I want to talk to her, to tell her I love her, to say good-bye. "Mommy! Mommy!" but she can't hear me.

The scenes were so vivid it was as if I were there. Little relief came when I realized it had been a nightmare, because I knew I was living this dream.

I worried constantly about what the end would be like. Would she linger? Would she slip into a coma? Would I watch her fade away in a hospital bed with those tubes and repulsive smells? I couldn't bear it. Even sleeping pills didn't help.

Spiritually, I cringe to confess, I was back at square one. I knew there was a God. That, unfortunately, was about the extent of my confidence. It was like starting all over again in my faith. It was awful trying to sing and minister in that torn frame of mind. Some nights the most spiritual thing I could say to an audience was simply I believed "there is a God." Some people must have gone away from my concerts wondering about the shallowness of my comments. It was an unsettling period, but I was so intent on not saying anything I couldn't stand behind with my life. I didn't want to be a hypocrite. We had always been committed to having a ministry that was known for its integrity.

I was confused over conflicting signals I received from speakers and writers on the subject of gratitude during turmoil. Does one really thank God for trouble? Call me unspiritual, but I had trouble with this. Handicaps, divorce, illness, death—were these really gifts in disguise from a loving Father who knows what's best for us?

I have struggled with that concept for years. When Ron and I faced infertility, we benefited by gaining a deep sensitivity for others in the same situation. It also made us more conscientious, grateful parents. But was barrenness *really* a gift from God? Was He the giver of it, and was I to actually thank Him for it? I was still working through that question, even though I had two children.

My faith wouldn't allow for doubts and questions about God. I had painted a picture in my mind of a Judge who could not tolerate questions. Doubting thoughts were quick and fleeting in this uncharted territory. They were reflective of deep struggles I was not ready to confront.

I felt guilty both blaming and yet trying to thank God for the terror and grief in my life. I wasn't comfortable questioning the image of God that was portrayed in my beliefs, but I didn't dare abandon my faith. I knew there was a God to whom I would someday be accountable, and for the time being I needed to trust the system. How dare I question His right to do what He wanted, including taking my mother.

Most hurting people will, at one time or another, struggle with their prayer lives, and I certainly did. Shock, numbness, and denial altered my ability to know how to pray and for what to pray. It wasn't that I didn't know what I wanted; I knew that all too well. But was a miraculous healing of my mother in God's perfect will? If it were not, dare I pray for it?

Often I struggled wordlessly. I could not begin to unravel the knot in my heart enough to convey what I felt. My only comfort lay in one of the many roles of the Holy Spirit. The letter to the Hebrews describes Him as a prayer partner. I hung onto the truth that the Holy Spirit would interpret the state of my heart, translating wordless frustration and anguish into spiritual needs.

I learned the difficult lesson that nothing magnifies the cracks and erosions in my faith more than trying to "perform" that faith under pressure. When the crucial foundational stone in our relationship to God is out of place, even the strongest incentive to glorify God in our pain will weaken. That one foundational truth must be intact; we must be sure of where we stand with God. We must know that we are cherished as His children.

As I began to painfully unravel the packaging around my faith, I saw it needed major restructuring in the understanding of God's love. I had to move past being loved in some theologically vague sense as in the fact that God loves everything and everyone He created. No, I had to learn that I, Christine Wyrtzen, am a jewel to God—that I am a cherished person. I had to get settled once and for all that God's love is truly unconditional, that He would not change His view of me, regardless of how I respond to crisis.

God does not send trauma and then sit back to see if we respond biblically. His love and support is not calculated to be in proportion to our performance. At that time in my life I needed above all else to reaffirm that my faith was an unshakable relationship, that it was not a code of conduct dictated by some man-made rule book.

Often a person who does not know that he is cherished by God lives his life strictly out of obligation, thinking that God will only love and accept him if He sees a good performance record. This kind of thinking caused a deep chasm in my life that completely robbed me of joy. There are subtleties here that are extremely important. An inability to come to grips with the way God sees us can make the difference between emptiness and joy, thus affecting every detail of our lives.

Time in the valley was revealing that the whole foundational basis of my faith was faulty. If someone were to ask why God saved me, I would have said something like, "He looked at the condition of my fallen heart and was grieved. Because He could not look upon sin, He adopted me and loved me for who I could become in Him." (Notice my answer did not say "for who I was" but "for who I could become.")

Instead of seeing the cross as a symbol of love and sacrifice, I saw it as a reminder of the need for work and daily cleansing. In my mind the cross was a way for me to rid myself of the sin that would continue to separate me from fellowship with God. Therefore, my Christian life was wrapped up in concepts like discipline, conscientiousness, diligence, servanthood, transformation, and death to self.

You may say, "Wait. Those are biblical concepts." Yes, they are, but they are to be balanced in a healthy, Christ-centered relationship. Apart from that, they are law —not life. That need to become, to be more acceptable, motivates with an obsession toward discipline, diligence, and servanthood. That was all I saw of value to God in my Christian life.

At the root of this issue was the question "How can God love me now if He wants me to spend my life trying to become more like His Son?" I knew the basics of salvation, but I still believed I was on a performance trip, that I would have to continually change myself to conform to the image of His Son if I were to feel His continued acceptance. That created a deep-seated insecurity. Biblical application became desperate and a necessary means of survival. Rather than living a life of obedience out of love for a God who deeply loved me, I was working feverishly for His approval, which would be measured by how I was "becoming." I didn't dare slip up, for the chance that my life might be over was at stake, and I would have to face the Lord.

I dreaded the moment when I would have to meet His eyes. I didn't want to see a hint of disappointment and hear, "Oh, Christine, if only you had been more committed, more disciplined."

To look forward to meeting Him with any confidence, I would have to be ever on my spiritual toes. I couldn't see how unbalanced all of this was until much later.

What pressure I had created for myself! A prolonged crisis, like the one I was enduring, rattles the skeletons in our theological closets. The painful issues were coming to full display for me to see. In my case, in my frenzied life of God-pleasing, there was no room for doubt, for anger, or for questions—no, not even for healthy evaluation of God's plan for my life. I didn't have the courage to be human and risk God's disapproval.

I didn't intend to give a false impression, but I'm sure there were those who knew my mother was dying, heard me speak at concerts, and believed I was holding up remarkably well. I tried not to be hypocritical. Yet I could not drag the mess of my emotions out in public and admit that I was tying myself in knots.

Entering the Studio

Recording studios are unique places, quite different from the rest of life. They are void of many trappings. The studio room itself often lacks carpeting, fancy furniture, and pictures. Clocks are rarely displayed, and one quickly loses track of time.

When one begins to experience profound pain, he also feels suspended in time. His life becomes focused on the simple things. Veneers are quickly peeled away to reveal whatever contents rest in the heart.

Time seems to stand still as long-range career and family goals give way to immediate needs. Next year is no longer anticipated. Today and tomorrow become extremely important. Plans on calendar pages give way to redefined priorities, and in many cases, simply survival.

7

In 1983 Ron and I made the decision to leave the employ of Word of Life. We would still live in Schroon Lake, but on January 1, 1984, Ron's resignation would go into effect, and we would both be full-time in our music ministry. It was a major decision for us, considering Ron had grown up at Word of Life. We had come to Christ through its ministry, and my music had found an outlet there.

We knew it was the right decision. It was time to break away, to be fully on our own. I was still struggling with my mother's impending death, although I was thrilled with the borrowed time that allowed us to enjoy her longer.

No one is ever fully prepared for death, but I tried to remain as objective as I could. I knew it would come, and I kept trying to tell myself that I was as prepared as I could be. I had read about it and talked about it from the platform. It would be difficult, but it could be handled.

Then came the unexpected. On the day that Ron's resignation became effective, we were busy celebrating the New Year with his family. Despite their demanding schedule across the country, Jack and Marge Wyrtzen had always made a commitment to be home for the holidays. Marge's signs of improved health made the festive activities more memorable. She had been ill most of her life. She and Jack had been told by a renowned physician on Long Island that she might not live past age thirty—and would certainly never survive childbirth. Though the birth of each was difficult, she eventually bore five children.

After church on that New Year's evening, they made their way to a friend's home. As Jack pulled in the driveway, Marge complained that she was having trouble breathing and asked to be taken to the doctor. Within seconds, she laid her head on her husband's arm and died. The life squad tried reviving her on the way to the nearest hospital but could not. We were called at home minutes later.

How unpredictable life is. Ron's mother had been of such support to us. She was consistently inquiring about the needs of my dad and mom; all the while, none of us realized that we would lose her first.

We couldn't understand God's sovereignty in all of this. How could He possibly have our best interest at heart when He chose to take both of our mothers within such a short period of time? What a crushing blow. Ron, strong and supportive in my crisis, was now the one in need. It had been he who cushioned the insensitivity of some while helping me recognize and appreciate those who really tried to extend comfort. Now he needed me to play that important role for him. I hoped that I would be as steady a force for his equilibrium as he had been for mine.

Six months later, while still grieving over our first loss, I noticed that my mom's health took a distinct turn for the worse. She had lost weight and energy, and she slept most of the day between meals. She had great difficulty getting up and down the stairs.

She no longer made comments like, "If I'm still here at Christmas, let's do this." She stopped caring about her clothes and rarely asked how the kids were doing in school. She seemed not to care about much at all. She had accepted her destiny. She wasn't angry. She was saying, in essence, "This has gone on long enough. I'm tired of living."

Late in the spring, we were in South Dakota for a two-day engagement, and the attendance the first night was poor. Except for a brief interview the next day, our time was free. To lift my spirits, and my mother's, I decided to call home. To get in the mood, I played a mind game with myself. Lately I hadn't enjoyed calling home. I felt out of touch, homesick. I was a long way from New York, and that's where I wanted to be. If Mom were having a difficult day, I would feel even worse. I didn't want to convey that to her, because I wanted this to be an uplifting call.

I tried to tell myself that handling bad news was no big deal. To prove this to myself, I flopped down on the bed, Indian-style, and dialed the number. She answered, which was unusual. She had to deal with coughing spells due to fluid build-up in her lungs, and speaking loudly over the phone almost always made them worse.

There was a slight lift to her voice when she realized it was me, and I was optimistic that the conversation would go well. I had rarely seen her despair, and she seemed happy I had called. The mood changed when she told me that she was having trouble with her vision. Cancer had invaded her pancreas, causing diabetic symptoms. Her blood sugar was up, and it was beginning to affect her eyesight. This made it hard to see people on the platform at church. It was interfering as she tried to read the newspaper. Her voice broke as she told me. This display of emotion was totally out of character for her.

I was flattered that she felt she could break down with me, because that was something she normally never did. But it was as if someone had shined a spotlight on me in that hotel room. There I sat cross-legged like a teenager, somehow thinking that my casual body language would lighten my response to the conversation.

The process of a loved one's death is a series of events. Each might find you at what you think is your limit. With this new piece of information from Mom, I thought once again that I had reached mine. I wondered if it could get worse, all the while knowing that it could and would. She would experience more regression, ultimately leading to death. My soul ached. The four walls around me seemed to replay the scene of the last several minutes. Was there no escape? I wanted out of the room. Out of the state. But where could I go that would bring relief from the awful sting of reality?

Was I supposed to thank God for this? Could I say with the hymn writer Horatio Spafford, who lost his family at sea, "It is well with my soul"? No. His story haunted me; things were *not* well with my soul. Sermons on thanking God echoed again in my head. Was God a cruel Father, standing over me, club in hand, demanding, "Come on, Christine! Thank Me!"? What would happen to me if I didn't perform?

Or was He a hurting and benevolent Father who watched cancer devastate one of His choice servants? Were His tears blending with mine? He was a man of sorrows, acquainted with grief. Jesus wept at the tomb of His friend, Lazarus. Here was the portrait of Christ to which I could cling. I needed a God from whom I could expect empathy, not judgment.

Mother telling me of her worsening condition only deepened my homesickness, but I was seeing something new in our relationship. She could be weak; she could show vulnerability.

Around this time Ron's brother gave me a book that changed the dynamics of my faith as it related to my struggle to thank God for Mom's cancer. Margaret Clarkson, in her book *Destined for Glory,* gives a fresh definition of gratitude in the midst of pain. She explains the vast difference between thanking God for my trials and thanking Him for walking with me through those valleys. To thank God for cancer would be to insinuate that He created it. How freeing to finally see disease as one of the many scars on fallen humanity. God allows the consequences of our sin, but He does not plan them. Eventually I was to find a deep well of gratitude from which to express many thank yous. I became overwhelmed by a God who would choose to share each detail of my experience and my mother's. That growth wasn't without setbacks, because becoming thankful takes time. In the throes of loss we find ourselves clinging to that which is threatened, unwilling to let go, no matter what the promised benefit. How ludicrous to even think of exchanging a mother for a wiser heart or for newly acquired eyesight!

After that difficult weekend in South Dakota, I had a terrible time working through the ramifications of what I had heard. I had expected my mother to grow weaker. Maybe I expected her to break down while talking to me, but I couldn't imagine her losing her eyesight. I honestly didn't think I could handle this. Though trying to work through those emotions, I was not successful at it.

One evening the phone rang. It was a friend who asked, seemingly sincerely, how I was doing. I breathed a heavy sigh. I decided to be honest and tell her about sitting on the hotel bed and calling home. I told her of the devastating news and how it had rocked me. After that long description, I summarized, "I don't feel capable of handling this."

Silence. Surely she heard me. Surely she's as overcome as I am. I waited. Finally she spoke. "I hear you're going to be in Michigan soon."

How I cringe to have to admit that her response occasioned the worst in me. *Wait till you need someone to talk to,* I thought. *Wait till one of your parents is dying and you reach out and make yourself vulnerable.* I didn't retaliate out loud.

*   *   *

Mother was also having to deal with others' insensitivity. She was at a stage where people were visiting her at home, wondering if this would be the last time they would see her. She was a master, however, at turning attention away from herself and onto them. She would insist they sit next to her and tell her all about themselves, what they were doing, what was happening in their lives. I learned, however, that if they never asked about her, she noticed it, remembered it, and would sometimes mention it later to our family.

A pastor friend drove several hundred miles to see her, yet he never even asked how she was feeling. Perhaps we should have concluded from his time and effort that he cared, but because he's a pastor, we all expected him to be concerned about Mom's feelings and attitudes. We had hoped he would be comfortable discussing these issues.

The Red Recording Light Is On!

The process of recording the music is called "laying down the tracks" and is the first visible sign of the finished product. As the players assemble and begin playing, their mind-set toward the song creates a "groove" stylistically. Defining this framework is crucial to the success of a song.

Our peaks and valleys greatly affect our attitudes about life. The wide range of emotional responses to both can best be identified and kept in balance by sharing them with the "players" in our lives. Teamwork builds the "groove" wherein we need to walk, which assures we will reach our goals.

8

Suffering purifies. When we are in pain, we are willing to let go of all that cannot stand the fiery test. We come to see ourselves for what we are —helpless, hurting, weakened by sin. We cry to God for wholeness, and this is the first step toward holiness.

Margaret Clarkson

I had been riding that thin border between anger and acceptance. Suddenly, for three days during the summer of 1984, I allowed anger the upper hand. I was a woman who needed to learn how to handle anger in a healthy way. My natural inclination always had been to repress it. I was the calm one. Displays of temper were for the less controlled person, not for me.

What a shock, then, for me and those around me, when I vented anger in a way that was foreign. I slammed car doors, heard myself raising my voice, and at one point threw a hairbrush across the room. For months I had done everything I could to stay teachable. I had used every ounce of energy to acknowledge my feelings before my God and to trust Him to keep my perspective healthy. But now my anger went unchecked. That was the excess baggage I took with me to Grand Rapids, Michigan, for a concert with Doug Oldham.

I had no idea that, during his portion of the concert, Doug would focus his music around the recent death of his father. He told of the last hours he had spent with his dad.

Doug was profoundly sad, and he was in turmoil, but I did not detect despair. What I saw was a man who delighted trusting a God who was his Friend. When Doug spoke of either his earthly father or his heavenly Father, his face radiated. Hearing and seeing that was like turning a mirror upon myself and being repulsed by the stranger with whom I lived. I didn't like her. I didn't know her. I wanted to turn my back on her and leave her behind.

After the concert, when nearly everyone else had gone, I found Doug in the sound room. I pulled him aside and managed only a few words. "Thank you for being used to change my heart tonight." That was all I could get out. He looked tenderly at me, and I sensed that he understood.

After a moment of silence he took my hands in his and asked God to remind me how much He loved me. He verbalized everything with which I was dealing. How refreshing to find someone who knew how to pray for me. After giving me a warm, fatherly hug, he made me promise to call him the day my mother died. It was a promise I was to keep.

Later that summer I visited my mother and for the first time since my phone call from South Dakota, I found her vulnerable. For a moment the tables were turned. I was the mother. She was the child. It was at the end of my visit, and I went over to where she lay on the couch. "Goodbye, Mommy," I said, leaning over her. She tried to sit up.

"Oh, just stay there," I said. "You don't need to get up."

But she pulled herself to a sitting position. I sat next to her and hugged her. When I went to pull away, I noticed she was shaking. I pulled back and discovered that she was crying. She said nothing, but I hugged her again, all the tighter. Frail and fading, she needed me. It was a totally new experience for this daughter, sweet and sad.

Some weeks later while on a flight from Dallas to Chicago, I was rehearsing that visit with her over and over in my mind to insure that I would never forget it. It was a beautifully clear day; the sky was virtually cloudless until halfway to O'Hare International Airport. It was then I noticed a haze developing. Nothing to worry about. Just a front like many I've flown through. I leaned back with my Walkman and closed my eyes. Twenty minutes later I began to feel uncomfortable. I opened my eyes to nearly total darkness at three o'clock in the afternoon.

Within minutes the sky was black, and the plane was bouncing. Even the flight attendants were buckled in. As the plane pitched, overhead compartments flopped open, luggage fell, and food scattered. It worsened as we continued to approach O'Hare. I expected pandemonium, but strangely there was a deathly silence. Many held hands. Others put their heads back and closed their eyes. Some pressed their faces against the windows, trying to find the source of the nightmare, the possible cause of impending death.

I prepared myself. I thought of my husband, my daughter, my new baby son. I thought of my mother eight hundred miles away. She had begun the process of dying nearly two years before. As I sat there, I experienced some of what Mom had verbalized—how her senses were sharpened and were focused on only the essentials of life. It seemed likely that we might crash upon landing and that all on board would die. I was scared, yet I remained outwardly calm. How ironic that I could precede her in death after all we had been through. How pleasant to realize that she could shortly be joining me in heaven. My mind flashed back to our embrace on her couch when I knew she needed me. Somehow it made my life more complete.

The landing was rough, but God spared us. In the terminal we learned that we were one of the last planes to land before the airport closed for several hours. Nineteen tornadoes had been spotted in the Chicago area that afternoon. All I wanted to do was call home. I had a close brush with death. I had accepted the prospect, uncomfortable about it only as I thought of Ron and the kids.

Unless God intervened and healed Mom, she would have no narrow escape like the one I had experienced. She was childlike when I had last seen her. In that moment I became the mother. Could I wish to have her life prolonged simply to satisfy my own need for a mother?

Maybe it was time to accept the final tickings of the clock. Her quality of life was obviously gone. If I could so easily accept my destiny with eternity, could I do any less for her?

Background Singers, Please!

Finally, it's time for words. The background singers come to help and support, to lend their encouragement. Their contribution adds variety and new textures to the song's message.

How quickly pain can make us lose perspective—and with it goes our determination to persevere. The ministry of encouragement can only occur in the presence of need. A well-timed word or caring gesture can help the wounded regain equilibrium. The background of encouragement supports those in need and provides new textures that build incentives for survival.

9

By repeating almost the same words about my mother in each concert, I was able to get through without breaking down. I had almost memorized it. That served as a defense mechanism against the pain. If I had to think about each word and the truth of it, I would not have been able to survive the constant reminders of her impending death.

If I had not mastered the delivery of the story, the implications would not have been so easily ignored. But I had to develop a callousness of sorts. During months of trying to deal with my personal pain, I also found myself dealing with that of others. In sincere attempts to let me know I was not alone, people told me their own stories of grief and of loss.

Post-concert conversations were filled with dozens of stories that demanded my full attention. I wanted to listen; I wanted to extend love, support, and encouragement. The result, however, was that I could not forget or put aside the many heartbreaking accounts no matter how I tried. When I consciously tried to push them out of my mind, they reappeared as nightmares, sometimes for weeks on end.

That forced me to further depend upon a detached account of mother's illness, which allowed me to somehow separate myself from reality. I was able to continue this without much emotional involvement until one night in Charlotte, North Carolina. It was the end of a series of concerts, and I was exhausted.

I confess I felt a little intimidated while preparing for that concert. It was held in the glassed-in dining room of a large, influential church. They had an extensive artist series, and I knew they had probably seen and heard nearly every type of program. I knew I would have to be on top, at my best, if I would truly minister to this audience. I was afraid that this would not happen if, in my fatigue, I relied on any memorized dialogue. Every comment would be fresh and unrehearsed.

I changed the order of the music and came up with new introductions. I didn't anticipate the results. I struggled for composure the whole evening. Fortunately, the audience of more than a thousand was warm and understanding.

When I tried to tell about my mother without the support of a learned script, the awful truth crept in, and I began to choke up. I had two songs to go, and I had no idea how I would make it. Finally, I stopped mid-sentence and broke down. It may have been only a fifteen-second break in the program, but it felt like fifteen minutes.

Somehow I pulled myself together enough to stumble through the song "Carry Me." But I couldn't go on. I stepped down off the stage, which was in the round, but couldn't find a seat. The pastor immediately went to the microphone and extended his hand so that I would join him. "Let's all join hands, and Christine and I will come down and stand among you as you pray silently for her, for her mother, for her family."

Some in the auditorium wept. At one point during the prayer, I looked up and was struck by the beauty of the scene. The gold from the sunset beamed through the windows and illuminated the large circle of people praying for me. Because I was so moved and encouraged by their gesture, I had the strength to finish the concert. I had a fleeting thought that if only an unbelieving person could see the love being shown, he would surely be drawn to Christ. The scriptural principle of the world identifying us by our brand of love would have proven true that evening. An atheist would have had to come to grips with a living God should he have witnessed the scene.

Perhaps our testimony to a fallen world has lost some of its credibility. We no longer love as we should. As members of the Body of Christ we are a family, yet we have not maintained the essence of a home. If a man's wife has cancer, he doesn't say, "Sorry, honey, but this is a new one on me. You'd better not count on me for comfort. I'll pray that someone better qualified will reach out to you."

That's an oversimplification, of course, but is that not akin to how the family of God neglects its own hurting neighbors? What do people in pain want from us? Just simple things. Practical things. Things that will help to carry them through.

They don't always want answers. At least not from us. Yet we feel under pressure to know what to say; we seem to want to impress them with our knowledge. And so we linger tongue-tied in the wings, waiting to be struck with a flash of brilliance. Often the wounded simply crave a silent partner with enough love to quietly wait out the storm.

Joseph Bayly, who lost three young sons at different times and under different circumstances, once said, "Comfort is a lost art, except for choosing a greeting card." Even then, care must be exercised. Get-well cards are wrong for the dying, of course. Thinking-of-you cards are better, but nothing means as much as that homemade card that evidences personal time sacrificed to construct a word of encouragement and greeting. You don't have to be skillful, and you certainly don't have to be an artist. If you have minimal creative ability, even adding your own note to a store-bought card or underlining the key words for emphasis can be meaningful.

An acknowledgment that you don't know what to say can be comforting. Somehow such genuineness is soothing. Those cards aren't quickly discarded. I know; I have a drawer full of them.

When an illness is prolonged, a succession of cards may not seem enough. In that case, it is good to find out the interests and hobbies of the one you're trying to encourage. My mother was a lover of nature, particularly wildflowers. We planned ahead to take her to one of her favorite stores where she could gather silk or dried flowers to arrange. When her health prohibited such outings, we brought the fixings to her. As she became weak and lacked the initiative to tackle a simple arrangement herself, we made it for her and surprised her with it. Rounding the corner of the living room with an arrangement in our hands always made her face light up.

Music can also minister where words can't, especially when pain dulls the ears to speaking. Determine the tastes of the music lover. It is important to keep their likes and dislikes in mind.

Any real effort to become involved in a hurting person's life will require more than a passing comment on the way out of church on Sunday morning. How much better to get a call in the middle of the week than to hear the same old "How are you feeling?" after church.

If you truly want to walk beside a hurting person, you must be willing to come to grips with your own mortality. Someone who overlooks his own discomfort will likewise look past another's. One of the things I found so distasteful about owning up, about facing my mother's impending death, was that I could no longer pretend that bad things happen only to other people. Havoc and heartbreak are part of my world as well.

We must expand our vision to include suffering in our daily lives. Such expansion is costly. Know in advance that permanent discomfort is part of the price. It is an awareness that is bittersweet. No longer will our eyes enjoy only that which makes us feel good. With our expanded vision, we consciously look upon that which hurts. But the fiber buil into our character will result in an inner strength that makes it possible for us to sit beside a broken friend or loved one. There will no longer be that urgency for the hurting person to recover so that we can feel more comfortable, less awkward.

Top: Christine's childhood home in upstate New York.
Bottom: The view of the village of Petersburg, New York,
from the Hewitt home.

Top left: Christine and Nancy (right), engaging in one of their
favorite pastimes.
Bottom left: Sitting on Daddy's knees.
Top right: Christine
Bottom right: With Nancy (left)

Above: Nancy
Top right: Christine's mother as a teen-ager.
Bottom right: Christine's mother at Thanksgiving dinner
before she was diagnosed.

Mrs. Hewitt with Jaime, one week old.

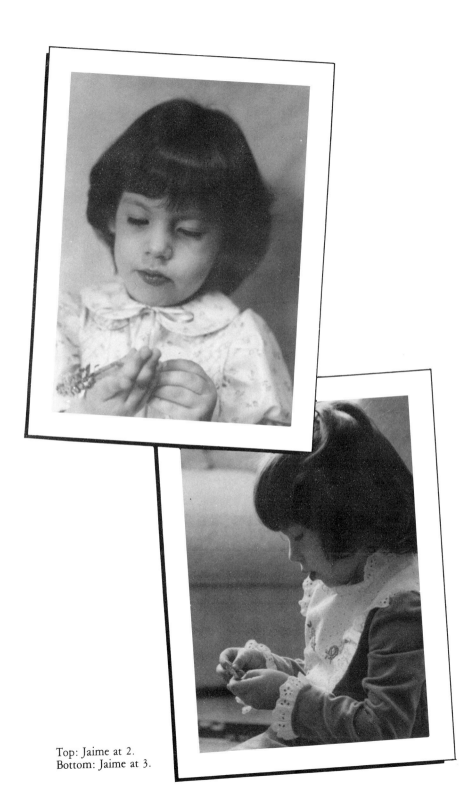

Top: Jaime at 2.
Bottom: Jaime at 3.

Ryan's first birthday party with Grandma and Jaime.

Ryan enjoying music at 9 months.

Easter Sunday, 1982.

Jaime at 3, with friend, age unknown.

Composing at home.

In the studio.

Above: The Hewitt's, sixth and seventh from the left (back row) on Germany trip.

Ron and Jaime (then 3).

Christine and her 3rd grader.

If you have been drawn to these pages because you are in a valley, let me encourage you to avoid the temptation to sit and wait for the right person to say or do something to genuinely help you. If we measure others with a scorecard, we can become bitter people. At best, there may be only one hour in your day when someone reaches you and temporarily helps to alleviate your pain and loneliness. That may make you feel better for a few minutes, but for the other twenty-three hours you might be alone again.

Only one Person can consistently reach down, put His arms around us, and give us the empathy our souls crave. How ironic that so many times we run from the very Person who can give us everything for which we long. We run elsewhere, desperately trying to fill the void with poor substitutes. Often Christians look for relief from other Christians, forgetting that even God's chosen are inherently sinful and are not capable of consistently exhibiting God's empathy.

Only He can love us without reserve. Only He can alleviate the intense loneliness that plagues all His creation. Only He has the arms to carry us over the long haul, for not only is He strong enough, but He sees the end of the road.

> My family has come with words to console,
> And friends have been calling on the telephone.
> In spite of the well-meaning words they've all
>   given,
> I can't help but feel that I'm standing alone.
> Lord, I do have some feelings I want to confide.
> I feel so alone though my friends offer smiles.
> It's only Your love that can carry the hurt;
> May I ask You to hold me for a few painful miles.
> Carry me, carry me,
> Won't You carry me now?
> I'm too weak and fragile to walk on my own.

I'll rest in Your love till once more I can stand,
To journey beside You and follow You home.[1]

Loneliness is the door that leads to an encounter with God that can deeply personalize our faith in a new way.

1. Words and music by Christine Wyrtzen. Used by permission of Loveland Music.

Last Minute Changes

At this stage in the recording process, a final evaluation occurs. Judgments are rendered on the tracks and background vocals. Checks are made on possible notes that are off pitch or completely misplaced. When all is deemed pleasing, the procedure continues.

We should be as attentive to people. The ever-changing human heart is in constant need of meticulous care. Relationships need frequent cultivation and nurturing to grow to potential.

Each moment, each seemingly casual contact, can have eternal consequences. Words wisely spoken can build a bridge strong enough to support any truth.

10

By now I was seeing my mother as frequently as I could get away. I saw her briefly in mid-October, then, a week later, I called her to let her know we were leaving the next morning for a few days of concerts. Before I had a chance to say anything, she broke in, "I hope this is a call to say you're coming down for the day."

"Well, no, I really wasn't. I was just calling to say good-bye before we all go on the road tomorrow. Why? Do you want me to come?"

"Well," she said, "would you consider coming down, just for today?"

She sounded so strong, healthy, and in such good spirits that I wanted to make the extra effort to go. It was uncharacteristic of her to ask for anything, so I couldn't even consider denying her request. I packed the motor home for the trip to the Midwest, talked with Ron, coordinated our plans for leaving later the next day, and then left immediately with our daughter Jaime for the two-hour drive south to Petersburg.

I was encouraged as I traveled that day, lifted by the healthy voice I had heard on the phone. Good days were few, and I found myself looking forward to the hours I would have with her that evening. If only the enthusiasm she had communicated that morning would still be present when we arrived.

It was. We found her at the kitchen sink, preparing dinner. She looked tired, but I expected that at five o'clock. She seemed especially glad to see us. She was even strong enough to enjoy Jaime's childish antics during the meal.

Dad had a meeting at church that night, so the three of us sat and chatted for hours. I played the piano so Jaime could sing her kindergarten songs for Grandma. I had brought a new women's magazine, which I shared with her. She leafed through it as we talked, frequently commenting on how good the pictures of the food looked. She was particularly struck with the photo of a gorgeous chocolate cake. "After you go to bed, I'll bake it for you," I said, fully expecting her to brush aside the offer.

I was stunned when she said she'd like that. I told her I had brought several pounds of red and green peppers to make a relish I knew she'd love, and she said she'd like for me to make that, too. Glancing at clothes in the magazine, she remarked how much trouble she had finding clothes in her closet that fit anymore.

"I'll drive you over to Vermont in the morning," I suggested, figuring I'd still get home in time to start our trip.

"If I feel up to it," she said. "We'll see in the morning, Chris." She added unexpectedly, "If I'm not here for Christmas, you won't let it spoil the holidays for you, will you?"

"Well, uh, we'll try not to," I managed. "Obviously, it won't be the same, but we'll do our best." My mind was racing. *Why is she saying this to me?* She had become so casual with the subject of death. She could ask my dad to get some milk, and then in the next breath talk to us about not being around for long.

"Oh, and in case I'm not here for election day," she said, "I've already cast my absentee ballot."

Not here? What is that supposed to mean? She had just had an incredibly good day, fixed dinner, planned a morning of shopping, and now she was saying that she might not be here for election day—in two weeks. I didn't even want to think about it. It didn't make sense. I had to brush her comments aside.

The heaviness left as quickly as it had come, and we returned to lighter subjects. We had some more fun with Jaime, and then we told stories from my childhood and hers, reveling in the laughter. I looked at the clock. Nine-forty. I couldn't believe it. Boy, did this feel great! I couldn't remember the last time she had stayed up past nine, let alone when she looked and acted so healthy and energetic. I didn't even mind that I would be getting to my baking and cooking projects so late. It was a privilege to do something for her that would have so much appeal.

We had talked for more than four hours when she finally sighed and called me by the nickname she'd given me as a child. "Well, Christletine, I think I'll go to bed." She pecked me on the cheek and made her way upstairs. With my spirits high, I worked in the kitchen until late into the night.

When Dad came home, he told me he had an early prayer meeting the next morning but would be back in time for breakfast. "OK," I said, "I'll have breakfast ready, and we'll wait to eat until you get back." We talked briefly about how much fun the evening had been, and he smiled. He said that he was grateful to have someone there with her so he could get out for a little while. We all, including my mother, knew how much he deserved moments like these. No one had been more attentive to a wife's needs than he. He never complained. One never saw him despair; there was only a determination to give her the best days possible, whatever that required.

Hope can often be found in the places we least suspect. Our senses must be continually sharpened to catch the unobvious, the nuances, the passing tones of daily life. It is here that we may find our greatest confirmation that God is on our side; His timetable takes into account our frailty. Throughout the next twelve hours, I was to be continually reminded of this truth.

83

I had found hope and incentive in the obvious places, one of which was a Scripture. It reminded me that all struggle is temporary. The words of the apostle Paul assured me that my deepest hurt would one day be productive as God would help deepen my ministry to others.

What I didn't know, as I wearily trudged up to bed that night, was that I was being singled out by a loving Father who wished to reinforce to me His involvement in my life.

I was home in my childhood bed. After all the turmoil, all the struggle, all the agony, I felt privileged I had seen my mother at her best for a few hours. My child slept on the floor next to me. From the bedroom just down the hall, I could hear my mother's labored breathing.

A sick person's breathing and nighttime coughing spells can be unnerving to hear. Eventually, I adjusted to the sound and slept.

A Moment to Treasure

Each challenging phase of the recording process is often preceded by a brief time to regroup. It offers one a chance to catch his breath before plunging into what's ahead. This time often results in additional productive ideas.

Our heavenly Father knows just when we need time to rest for a moment, reflect, and be reassured that He is deeply involved in our lives. Sometimes we just need to be held before we feel strong enough to continue.

11

I was awakened at seven by Jaime's stirring. She was still asleep, but I knew immediately what had disturbed her. From Mother's room I heard labored wheezing, a tremendous intake of breath followed by a long sigh. Then another, and another, and another. Then silence. I was so glad the breathing had not degenerated into the hacking, rasping cough that would have awakened her.

I shuddered. A chill overwhelmed me. How long would she have to suffer? When the stillness returned, Jaime settled back down, and her own breathing became deep and regular. I slipped out of bed to see if Mom needed anything. I pulled on a robe and tiptoed down the hall; her door was open a crack. I didn't dare push it for fear a squeak would interrupt her sleep.

Through the crack, I could see her face was turned away from me. I knew my dad was at church and would be home soon, so I decided to get a head start on breakfast. I crept downstairs and into the kitchen where her cake waited on the counter and the Italian relish sat in the refrigerator. Also on the counter were the stark reminders of Mom's illness: several bottles of pills, glycerin stix to test blood sugar, and syringes.

I heard the car pull in. In a moment the kitchen door opened. "Good morning, Chris," Daddy said. "How's Mother this morning? Hear any movement up there?"

"She's still sleeping."

"Good," he said. While we were talking, I heard Jaime come down the stairs and begin playing in the next room. Dad peeked over my shoulder at the simmering pots on the stove.

"She woke us earlier with her breathing," I said.

He nodded grimly. "Christine," he began, his voice thick, "I have to tell you that I recently came to the place where I can't wish her to stay with us any longer." I turned toward him, unable to speak. There was a long silence; he needed for me to answer him.

"Where are you on this, Chris? Do you know what I mean?"

I nodded. "I came to the same place several weeks ago on that dangerous flight to Chicago. I had to finally acknowledge, that for her, there is no consistent quality of life anymore."

He shook his head in agreement as I turned back to the stove. We were admitting that we had finally grown in our ability to accept her death. It wasn't pleasant to talk about, but it was necessary. It was healthy. I am so glad he had admitted his feelings first, because I had planned to tell him how I felt, but I wasn't sure of the timing. We both accepted the inevitable. It was a major step.

He complimented me on the cake sitting before him on the counter.

"I think I'll check on her," he said.

"Don't wake her just for breakfast," I said. "She can come down later, or I can take something up to her." He disappeared around the corner and started up the stairs.

I finished setting the table and moved back to the stove. I heard Dad's footsteps descending the stairs. His steps were slower than when he had gone up. He came into the kitchen stiffly, his face pale, and I knew. "Chris," he said, his eyes wide, "Mother's gone. Come."

As I approached her room this time, the door was wide open. She lay on the bed in exactly the same position she had been half an hour before. I realized then that I had apparently heard her last four breaths. I moved around to the other side and saw the ugly mask of death. Her face was contorted, discolored, without life. I hardly recognized this face; it was not the well-known window to the soul we had all loved so much.

It was no longer my mom. Yet, somehow, there was comfort here. Clearly she no longer resided in this body, and that gave me peace. I was overwhelmed with a sense of victory. After closing her eyes, Dad said, "I need to go and call the coroner." I nodded and heard him turn away.

I sat down on the bed and put my hand on her arm. "I love you, Mommy," I said. "And I'll miss you. But I'll be OK. I am so happy for you. Thank You, Father, for the special home you prepared just for her, and for me too. I can hardly wait to join her." The simplicity of that prayer surprised me. For a short time, the profound struggles of the past months gave birth to a childlike trust that carried me through the shock of the next few days.

While the sausages continued sizzling on the stove, I helped Dad with several phone calls; the hardest was to Nancy at school. When I finally returned to the kitchen, the cake, the relish, the breakfast I had cooked, and the fourth place setting at the table all spoke to me. So, this is what death is all about. October 20, 1984.

Although still in shock, the deepest part of my soul knew joy. The same God who raised the dead had made time for me. He had waited for me to verbalize my acceptance of her death. He had orchestrated an arrangement of that final morning that made room for my limitations.

Phone calls continued to be made and received. Many comments will always be treasured. Doug Oldham was once again encouraging. "Tell Christine that I love her and really understand her feelings right now because I've been there. And gently remind her that God will ultimately get the victory over death."

As the news spread, people began arriving—Ron, Ryan, Paula, and the pastor. We worked out travel details for Nancy to come from the West Indies. I held up fairly well, for death had seemed to happen gradually. She had lived much longer than originally anticipated, and then for a few days she was still within reach. For a couple of hours she lay upstairs, within sight and touch, until arrangements were made to move her to the funeral home. She was then made up cosmetically, as though she were still alive. I could still see her and touch her. Then she was moved to the church, where we held a service prepared for her. Nancy and I played numerous classical and sacred pieces on the piano and organ, and then Nancy accompanied on the piano as I played a flute solo of "Largo," by Handel, one of Mom's favorites.

Then came that final, cruel moment at the end of the service when it was time for all of us to journey a half-mile south to the familiar cemetery plot. Putting Mother in the ground was beyond what I thought I could handle. Now I was really losing her. The casket we had selected with such care would be put underground, never to be seen again. Mommy would no longer be in her bedroom upstairs, or in a parlor at the funeral home, or in the front of the church. She was about to be put beneath the frigid New England ground. My head acknowledged that Mom was really in heaven and that only her earthly shell was here—awaiting resurrection. But in my heart it didn't make sense.

The rest of the day was a blur. There was a large gathering at my dad's home. While friends and acquaintances milled around and enjoyed the buffet, I was preoccupied with the casket still under the tarp several miles away. The mortician would be there now, with his men, about to finish their job. Yet, as I mingled with people throughout the house, conversations reflected normal life. The incongruity just didn't fit.

When we returned home, I began to wonder if I were the only one aware of the loss. But then the cards and letters started arriving. How therapeutic some of them were! Paula wrote:

Christine and Ron,

Thank you for allowing me to walk with you through this valley. I went to Petersburg with the prayer that I'd be able to help you. Instead, I came away in awe. I learned by your example how to handle this experience. Now I pray if He ever asks me to walk this same road that I'll follow in your steps and do half the job you two did in paving the way for others. I love and respect you both.

From a couple who are good friends:

Dear Ron and Chris,

Once again we stood speechless—with full hearts—wanting to help you in your grief, yet not knowing what to say or how to say it.

It was a privilege to hear the tributes to your mom. It is a privilege also to observe your testimonies and see the examples of your lives . . . this year especially. We love you two and your children. Our prayers are with you as you travel.

And then from the new friend from Chicago, the woman who had handed me the long letter after the concert:

Dearest Friend,

I just wanted you to know that my heart has been heavy with care and prayer for you. I am thankful that it was simple and that your mom went in peace.

But how I grieve for you in your loss! Time is nonexistent in heaven, but it is often an unbearable commodity for us, as we wait below. For this goodbye, for all the love, for all the memories that are painful right now, I weep for you. I offer arms of love and prayer to encourage you as you walk through the lonely road of grief.

I pray that you will be able to grieve. Take the time to feel and realize your loss, so that your pain may one day be balanced by the preciousness of your memories. I hope you will be still and linger in the valley so that you may be restored to soar again in the peaks.

May God lead you and hold you as you grieve and mourn, and fill your heart with His presence.

I drank deeply from the well of encouragement that these friends offered. As was the case months earlier when we had lost Ron's mother, our family was numb and trying to live life normally when nothing was normal. We clutched these expressions of hope tightly to our hearts.

I had no concept of what I would soon be confronting. Acceptance of death does not take place at the funeral. I had been trying to prepare myself for two years for what death would really mean, thinking that acceptance would culminate at the moment she slipped out of this life. I was finding it was not so. I found I still had to work to make myself believe that she was indeed gone. This was so radical a concept that it was easy to keep the truth of it from entering my heart.

Time for the Lead Vocal

Finally, the singer walks into the tiny, isolated vocal booth to perform the song. Surrounded by glass, he stands alone, for all to see, to hear.

It's a solitary time. He begins slowly, carefully, to deliver the lyrics—the message. It's received and judged. It's accepted or rejected. And so the fine-tuning continues until the end product, the final vocals, pleases the one who sings and the one in charge.

The message our life sings is also a solo performance. Enhanced by melodies of family and friends, it remains a single statement. It's to be delivered by each one of us —alone.

12

We may soften the horror of death by honoring the corpse. We may patch it up, preserve it, dress it in going-away clothes, place it on a restful couch, and surround it with flowers. Shall we deny death and try to make it beautiful?

Joseph Bayly

I continued to practice denial, which was easy because my mother wasn't around to confront me with her illness. I didn't know it at the time, of course, but I had become diseased from overindulgence in repression. Something hurts? Repress it. Deny it. People practice this tactic until it is highly perfected. Your husband abuses you? It's all right; look at all the pressure he's under and how nice he is when he wants to be. Your wife is an alcoholic? It's not so bad. She's just sick. She could quit drinking whenever she wants. Your friend betrayed you? Who cares? You have plenty of other friends—and the Lord. Anyway, we're supposed to forgive.

We have all the scriptural answers, so we pretend these wounds don't hurt, that they don't matter. From childhood, we're taught to gloss over pain to the point that, if we're not careful, the habit will embed itself deeply into our lifetime response system. Denial is the response that keeps us from seeing and acknowledging reality.

My refusal to confront my emotions was evidenced in my reaction to others. A woman once commented, "Christine, what a shame that your kids will never know their grandmother." Had I been healthy and truly well-adjusted, I would have agreed with her. I would have said, "Yes, it is very painful for us. We wish it had been otherwise, and trust that God knows what He is doing."

But no. I said, "That's OK. Look at all the wonderful years we enjoyed having her with us." A nice sentiment, but it was not the feeling in the depths of my heart. The veneer of denial-based responses is thick and hard. It separates comfort from pain, for beneath that layer lies a heart that will do anything to avoid the painful truth.

I practiced denial when I avoided my mother's clothes closet after her death. When I chose not to use the blueberries she had picked and frozen. From somewhere inside a voice reminded me, *If you use them, she will not be here to replace them.* What I was really telling myself was that when they are gone, she is gone. What I couldn't admit was that she was gone already.

Some spend their entire lives choosing the path of denial. It does seem more comfortable, but there is a price. We can never appreciate God in all His sufficiency if we don't acknowledge that we are in despair. We come to cherish eternal hope only if we learn to truly embrace our fallen world. It is ugly at times, and one is better off to admit it.

One who chooses a life of denial is handicapped and is unable to comfort others. Rather, he meets them with cliches, bromides, and catch-all phrases. "Keep your chin up." "Things will look better in the morning." "Just keep trusting." "Look on the bright side." Such statements are of little encouragement. They alienate. How much better to admit to the grieving one, "I don't understand this, and I don't like it either. I hate to see you in pain, and I'll stand here with you until the storm is over."

Stop pretending that everything is OK when it is not. Yes, God is on His throne and will ultimately bring perfection to this world. But in the meantime, He can allow the effects of our fallen society to enrich the spiritual dimension of our lives if we allow Him to accomplish this. Things can work together for good—sometimes externally, and always internally if we are willing. But to deny pain, to deny grief, to deny despair is to live a lie. Force it to the surface, and then hang on to God for dear life.

I had only begun to recognize this truth as I drove home to Petersburg for the first time after my mother's death. The two-hour drive, alone through a powdery dusting of snow, gave me time to envision our house without Mom. I wavered, wondering whether or not to visit the cemetery first. Finally, I decided that avoiding it would be unhealthy. I would be repressing the awful truth. Mom was gone. I didn't want to postpone facing the inevitable.

The funeral and the burial had been endured in a haze. Reality faced me squarely as I was coming back to a house that used to be home for our family. I knew intellectually that the longer I put off facing her grave, the harder it would be to ever face the truth. I didn't realize then, of course, how deeply denial was ingrained in my psyche. Still, I decided to stand tall and make the trip.

It was still morning when I pulled onto the little dirt road. I was alone. The cemetery was empty and covered with a quarter inch of white. I wondered if I would be able to find the site without seeing the freshly turned soil. I located the Hewitt row of tombstones and noticed one grave where the dirt was still mounded. A simple marker stood where a new stone would eventually be placed. It read Gertrude Hewitt. How strange!

I was so accustomed to seeing her name on mail. I was reminded of her signature. Her name did not belong here amid relics. I shivered. Winter was settling in, solid and frigid. I felt sorry for her there in the ground, though I knew better. In the past I had shaken my head and chuckled at loved ones who wanted to take a blanket to the cemetery in the winter to cover their loved ones. It wasn't so funny now.

My mind still fought the truth, but I couldn't deny this. There was her name. There was her grave. In it was her body. She was gone. I would not be rehearsing this incident with her. I would not be sharing anything with her again. No smile. No joke. No tidbit. No recipe. No conversation. Her name was on the marker. That was truth. That was reality.

Helplessness gave way to frustration. I hated this. I had no control over death. I couldn't change it. Surprising myself, I lashed out, kicking the marker with all my strength. Then I cried. That brought relief. "Well," I finally muttered, "did you like your youngest daughter's behavior?" I pictured a chuckle from her. Somehow I knew she would understand.

The next few weeks brought countless flashbacks to that scene. The confirmation of her death, underscored by the discovery of her gravestone, highlighted all sorts of new admissions. I knew far less about my mom than I cared to acknowledge. Unanswered questions nagged at me. I had really believed before her death that we were a tight, close-knit family. But now, as I had to deal with the admission that I had less information about my mother than I would have liked, this further aggravated and complicated the grieving process.

The way I have painted the picture of my family is the way I truly believed it was—intimate. But I began to think of things I didn't know about her. Things I had never asked her. I couldn't remember why I hadn't. Was there some distance between us that I hadn't detected before? I'm not referring to deep, dark questions of intrigue. I'm talking about the general, typical questions family members would ask each other.

I knew she had had a traumatic childhood. I knew her house had burned down when she was little. She had a difficult relationship with her father, who disowned her when she married. My grandmother had suffered with cancer, and my mother had been by her side when she died. She didn't cry at the funeral, but later she would choke up at the mention of her mother's name.

Was there a reason we never talked of certain feelings, memories, and conclusions? Isn't it fairly typical for mothers and daughters to discuss these things?

Dreams returned. Not nightmares as before, but strange, weird dreams common to the bereaved. Mother had come back. She was alive. Once I dreamed I had gone home to visit Dad, and as we sat at the breakfast table, Mom walked in. We were shocked, surprised, and thrilled. We began catching up on our lives since she'd been gone, even telling her about the presidential election. What a disappointment to wake up from dreams like that. I tried to go back to sleep to recapture the moment.

I began to assess my childhood. I thought about my relationship with Nancy. As sisters, and as a family, were we really as close as the Rockwellian tales I had told myself? Sure, we'd been happy. There had been no real trauma. But was there heart-felt communication? Were Nancy and I as close as I thought? Did I really know her? How was she reacting to all of this?

Before Nancy returned to school in the West Indies, I made plans to visit. I spent four days alone with her at the end of the semester. Most of the time we sat on the beach talking. For the first time in my life, I felt we really communicated. It was a shock to learn how deeply depressed she had been over Mom's illness. She told of how she had run the beaches and cried, unable to concentrate on her studies.

She had never shared this with me before. I recognized for the first time how much she was alone, and I had to confront that, for whatever reason, she hadn't confided in me.

My heart broke as I listened to my sister. I now had to admit that, no, we were never as close as I had believed. I had thought she had all the answers, was completely self-reliant, and in need of no one. We were different in so many ways. Family and friends had come to recognize Nancy's strong, determined spirit as a reflection of a heart without need, whereas my gentle, less assuming ways were seen as a sign of weakness. I was presumed to be the fragile china doll type in need of protection. These differences had further alienated us.

Our strengths and weaknesses were different and yet the same. We needed each other. Ironically, the separation from our mother drew us together. Now we are deeply involved in each other's lives. We really talk, listen, and experience the kind of relationship that we wish we had developed as children.

My time in the West Indies was productive. It introduced me to a real person who also happened to be my sister. I flew home and prepared to get ready for our next concert tour. I had to prepare for Jaime's home schooling, make the motor home livable, and tie up loose ends around the house. But energizing all of this activity was the newly born friendship between Nancy and me.

Ron, the children, and I had been traveling in ministry for a year. Jaime was five, Ryan two, and most of our days were spent in our motor home. To this day when Ryan sees one on the road, he wishes we could trade in our present life-style. We loved being together.

We decided with the amount of traveling we were doing to move to Cincinnati. It didn't make sense to stay in upstate New York when it took so long to travel to and from most of my concerts. Cincinnati is more centrally located, the place where my office is, and is a city that I have always loved. It would truly get us out on our own. In many ways it was a dream come true for me—to work more closely with Paula and the staff, to be involved with a wonderful church there, and to interact more often with people I had grown to love. Ron and I were confident that this was a wise choice for us, and we moved with the peace that God had led us to a place that was good for us in every way.

The unseen problem was that stress points had arisen in our lives. Ron had experienced a significant job change within the past year. His mother had died a year before, and mine two months earlier. Now a major move. I was an all-star on stress charts, headed for trouble without even knowing it.

At first I blithely cruised along, performing in fifteen concerts a month, traveling, home schooling, working with the ministry. Nagging at me, however, was the baggage that I faced inwardly every day—the grieving process involving both mothers, the re-evaluation of my relationship with my mother, and the effort to come to grips with those who had criticized me for my life-style. Were they right? Was it heartless or egocentric for Ron and me to take our children with us all over the country for the sake of ministry?

My self-confidence was flagging. I missed my mother terribly. I didn't like the doubts about my past, and although in many ways we were a model family, there were barriers, walls of silence between us.

For six months I ran on nervous energy. There seemed to be no resolution to the inward struggle in my mind. Things were not coming together. The positive move and change of location to Cincinnati had not distracted me or cushioned me from dealing with these issues.

In the midst of these internal questions, Ron was offered a job back at Word of Life. It was a job he had really wanted. We were confused. With the state of unrest in our souls, we were overwhelmed by the decision facing us. We prayed earnestly that God would show us His plan by making the issues black and white. He did. The door to Word of Life was closed.

Then Ron pursued and was offered a job in New Jersey that greatly appealed to him. He had looked into it seven years before on a whim, but there had been no position available. He would head up a warehousing operation, distributing competition water-ski boats to dealers in seven Mid-Atlantic states. This job was tailor-made for him. He was familiar with this line of boats, having been exposed to them since he was seven years old. Being an expert slalom skier and barefooter himself, this job was a dream come true. Yet it meant another move after we had been in Ohio only six months.

Ron wanted to make the right decision, and he tried to get my input. I felt paralyzed. All I saw was another big move, yet I hesitated to tell him that the thought of a move overwhelmed me. I didn't want to stand in the way of his getting a job that was well suited for him. I know he would have turned it down if I had been honest, yet in many ways I didn't know what I wanted. There were too many other issues demanding my strength and concentration.

It was as though someone had just turned off the energy button, and I couldn't deal with it.

The Power in Control

Envisioning the potential of all the musical elements, the recording engineer is a master at fine-tuning the sounds of the instruments and voices to produce the most pleasing product. With dozens of knobs at his fingertips, he skillfully moves each with meticulous precision until all is well polished.

Our perspective on life and on the situations in which we find ourselves must be constantly evaluated. As we submit and become accountable to our heavenly Father, He is able to control, adjust, and work all things together for good.

13

When we learn to rest our souls in God's mighty truths, our suffering takes on eternal dimensions. Our pain may not grow less, our loss may not be restored, our griefs may still be ours, but their power to harm us is broken.

Margaret Clarkson

I didn't have the energy to make a decision, good or bad. My root system had crumbled, and I had grown beyond caring. I didn't know I had slipped into depression. Only a handful of people knew how serious it was, and they were troubled.

Ron didn't know what to do. My self-image had plummeted. I remembered the voices of criticism from my past and decided that maybe those people had been right. Was I a failure as a wife and mother? How could I stand on a platform and have anything worthwhile to say? I perceived these things to be true, and what one perceives to be true becomes truth to him, accurate or not.

I reasoned that Ron loved me too much to be honest with me in confirming my new beliefs about myself. I was unable to see at this point that I had become the ultimate people-pleaser, breaking my back to remedy everything anyone thought I was doing wrong, wanting everyone to like and accept me and my ministry.

You can never win when you get into that cycle. There is always someone who thinks you should be behaving in a different way, doing things differently, saying things differently. My numbness and inability to even identify my problem created walls of silence in our marriage that were difficult for Ron and me to handle. One of the strengths we have always had going for us is the rock-solid foundation of love and commitment.

Ron and I are not the loud, argumentative type. But the scary barriers of silence and misunderstanding can be equally as challenging. I felt worthless, and I'm sure he was frustrated beyond measure. But he would not give up. He would not leave me alone in my despair.

The turmoil in my mind deepened every day. While doing something as simple as cleaning up the breakfast dishes, something minute would set me off, and I might sit and stare out the window and tremble. I could not deal with anything out of the ordinary. Life looked bleak, hopeless, like an unending tunnel of trouble. I had no strength, no energy, no reserve to make even the smallest of decisions.

I was petrified. I was afraid that I was losing my mind, aware of the stigma surrounding the mentally ill. I had had little experience with anyone who had emotional problems, and the only person Ron knew of convinced him there was indeed cause to worry. All I knew was that sometimes pouring a cup of coffee and sitting at the table seemed like the only thing I could accomplish. I would sit there and stare at it, doubting I had the energy to lift it and take one sip.

I feared I had cancer. I was tired all the time. I looked drawn. My hair didn't shine. My shoulders were stooped. My usual healthy countenance had vanished, and I became convinced I would be the recipient of the ultimate bad news—my own terminal illness.

The worst part of the depression was that I couldn't turn back the clock to reverse the deaths and trauma that I suspected had caused my profound sadness. I was trapped. There was no way out. I had to look at my situation, deal with it, and either work through it and eventually find joy or live forever like I was. That was a nightmare beyond description.

In the past my problems had always allowed for easy solutions. No longer did this apply. I had snapped, like a slinky that had been sprung, and at that moment I believed I could never be put back together. If there were answers, I didn't know where to find them.

I felt spiritually bankrupt. It would take a while for me to see that my background had paved the way for me to live out my faith in a frenzied mode of God-fearing and God-pleasing. This would give evidence of a weakness in the basic philosophy of my relationship to God. I was the product of a limited view of my heavenly Father. Had I recognized this, I might have seen a life preserver bobbing at the surface; it would have offered a ray of hope.

The raging storm continued within me. I thought I was fighting for control of my mind and spirit. I felt as if I were drowning, and I couldn't tell what was pulling me under. I didn't know where to turn, but I knew I had to take a risk. We could only think of a few people who might understand and be able to help.

Ron was worried and tried everything he knew. He tried to get me to tell him what I was feeling and what I thought was wrong. I could only say that I didn't know. For the next three weeks he did most of the work around the house, insisting that I lie down if I didn't feel well. That became frequent. I felt guilty doing that to the man I loved, but I honestly couldn't change anything. I hardly spoke around the house, so consequently it wasn't long before my voice grew weak. I would sing half a song and become hoarse. The amount of crying I did wreaked havoc on my vocal cords. We had to cancel and reschedule several concerts because I simply couldn't sing.

I did know that the issue of my mother's death was one thing pulling me under. I was still in mourning, in deep grief over the loss of my mother. People told me that after a year my vision of my mother would change, that I would remember her more in times of health than illness. The memories would be sweet rather than bitter. I found that difficult to comprehend because I felt as if I would be doing my mother an injustice by grieving any less. Wouldn't I be minimizing her memory by saying that my grief was healing and that my loss was not as painful? Or that I could finally think of other things, that she wasn't the first and only thing on my mind when I awakened every morning?

It was as if I would be admitting that my love for her had lessened. I interpreted the depth of my grieving as a holy and righteous act. Perhaps I was proving something to myself and to her by missing her so intensely. I was in effect saying to her, "I miss you this much, and for your sake I won't get over it."

By this time I realized that I was in a depression so entangled that it would take a professional to help me. And so I turned to a Christian psychologist in the Midwest whom I respected and trusted.

An appointment was set, and the polite, kind, everyone-pleasing Christine showed up, ready for the quick fix. I didn't see that this very side of my personality was my problem. I didn't know that I had been denying my true feelings for years and had been covering them by trying to please everybody, including God, to win His favor. I thought I needed to shape up, and that when I met this man, he would sit behind a desk in a suit and tie, ready to open his Bible and set my life straight with prescribed scriptural formulas.

He was, however, not what I expected. He wore docksiders, khaki pants, and a polo shirt. Looking at him, I wondered if he were going to be able to give the help I had anticipated. He later told me that my very appearance revealed much about my condition. I was trying to maintain an image of the put-together saint who simply needed some cold, hard advice. Skirt, blouse, jewelry, Bible, notebook, and pen. I was so locked into doing what was expected of me. I came prepared to take notes and do as I was told.

The truth was that I was desperate to find answers. Although I feared at times that I was losing my mind, I really thought my problem was simply that too many things had gone wrong in my life. I wanted someone to assure me that the pain was over, and if no one could do that, I didn't think I would ever care about life again. I was looking to this man for answers.

The office was set up informally with two recliner chairs, a box of tissues on the corner of the desk, and an empty coffee mug next to one of the chairs.

"Let's sit and have a chat," he suggested. I was caught off guard. A chat? We were going to small talk? I sat down.

"Would you like some coffee?"

I noticed his cup was empty. "No, thank you."

"You really don't want any?"

"No, thank you."

"If you had wanted some, Christine, would you have said, 'Yes, I'd love some'?"

I thought, *What is this? I came in here to talk about my life falling apart, and he's quizzing me about coffee.* "Probably not," I admitted.

"Why not?"

"Because your cup is empty."

"Oh, I see. You don't want to put me out."

I shrugged. He continued, "I noticed you brought a notebook and a Bible. What were you hoping to receive from me, a quick fix with answers you could take home on a notebook pad?"

I nodded.

He continued quietly, reflectively, "You always do everything just right, don't you? You're on time today. You're all dressed up. In the concerts where I've seen you, you've always impressed me as being so sweet. So polite. I bet you always do the right thing and say the right thing, and you would die if you offended anybody. Is that right?

"Well, that depends. Is there anything wrong with that?" I asked.

"If you're denying what's inside you there is, Christine."

And we were off and running. He asked questions that brought periods of silence where I had to dig deep to find the answers. I discovered that I was a stranger to myself, inclined to give answers I thought to be correct rather than ones that reflected the real me.

When he understood my reaction to his offer of coffee, I knew I was in for a ride. He had touched a nerve. The very things people admired about me had become walls I erected that conveniently prevented me from being myself and risking rejection. For the first time I was about to discover the unconditional love of God. Excavation had begun. Faulty foundations were leveled, and with a clear view of the state of my heart, feeble steps toward a new beginning became possible.

Time to Mix

The "mix" is the crucial process that allows for all of the final adjustments. The instrumental and vocal sounds are fine-tuned. If a vocal performance is weak, the track can be "boosted" to help compensate. If the instruments come across too aggressively, their volume can be reduced to help maintain balance.

As we near the end of time in the valley, we can begin to anticipate the fruit that will result. We sense that previous misconceptions have been tempered by more accurate revelations. Our dependency upon man has been reduced, whereas our desire for God has been elevated.

14

Rooted in the Word of God, watered by the Spirit's dews, and warmed by our flickering faith, God's good seed begins to sprout.

Margaret Clarkson

Time with the Christian psychologist revealed that I had been doing people a disservice by not allowing myself or them to be human. Father, mother, husband, friend, pastor—it mattered not. I shifted uneasily in my chair as the counselor pointed a finger at people whom I loved. He gently introduced me to the possibility that they were less than perfect. I defended them zealously. He had not, of course, set out to insult people I cared about. It's just that he needed to bump me, to nudge me into reality so I could begin dealing with life. But I remained resistant to what he was saying.

We were at a stalemate. He stopped and backed up. "Tell me why you think you're here," he said.

"Because everything has gone wrong in my life." And I ran down all the losses I had experienced. He sat and looked at me. I said nothing. I am not one to talk when I have nothing to say. I think between sentences, and I don't feel obligated to fill silences. So I waited and looked back at him.

"Where does joy come from?" he asked thoughtfully. "Does joy come from things that are going right? Where do we find it?"

I confessed that I had no joy, so I was the wrong person to ask just then. "I know where it's supposed to come from," I said. He raised his eyebrows, as if to ask. "From God," I added.

"But you're not joyful."

"No."

"So, God brings you no joy."

"No. Not right now."

"Well," he said, "we can agree that there is a problem. We've got to find out why God doesn't bring you joy." We talked at length on that subject until one of his reactions jumped out at me like handwriting on the wall. "Maybe God doesn't bring you joy because you haven't really experienced His love. You haven't needed His love because you have made everyone in your life perfect. They never fail you. Only those who face the fact that we live in an imperfect world and with inadequate people can really come to know God and experience His love. That brings us joy. You have had this intricate support system. You haven't needed God."

He was talking about denial. I had been denying reality for so long that I was even denying that I was in denial.

It was difficult for me to admit that people could be human. I believed everything everyone told me was right, and I was wrong. Life was easier to control by being the one who could always change. If someone criticized me, I assumed I was wrong. The way to fix it was simply to change my behavior.

We talked for several more hours. At the end he told me something that relieved me and refreshed me like a spring of crystal-clear cold water in the middle of a desert. "In many ways, your perceptions about life are right on target. You are probably one of the most emotionally healthy people I've seen in a while."

He wasn't telling me I was OK. Clearly, there was room for growth, but he was assuring me that I hadn't lost my mind, that I hadn't lost touch with reality. He assigned me the task of examining my own faith, of putting on paper why I thought God had saved me. It was he who made me see that my entire concept of the love and judgment of God had given me a warped system of belief and practice from which to live out my faith.

"This system," he said, "has made it convenient for you to close the door on dealing with several problems. Our job is to unlock those doors and send you away to walk through them and deal with what you find on the other side."

It would be a journey of more than two years, and I would see that counselor only one more time, just to establish that I was on the right track. The only prediction he made that troubled me was that I would get worse before getting better. I had to shed the illusion that my childhood was Pollyanna perfect. No one's is. I had to stop believing that everyone in my life was perfect. It wasn't fair to me or to them to lay that burden upon their shoulders. Knowing that fact alone was the start of identifying many similar problems in my thinking, and I began looking at things in a healthier way.

One of my main problems was that I did not have the kind of faith that allowed me to be angry. That's why, even in the midst of seeing my mother deteriorate and die, I was outwardly angry for only three days. I couldn't afford to offend God. I needed His acceptance. And I never saw the incongruity between the fear of offending Him by my actions and the fact that He loved me and saved me while I was yet dead in trespasses and sins.

You can't imagine the freedom I've felt in learning that I can make mistakes. I can blow it. I need to make things right, of course. I need to apologize if I've hurt someone. Knowing that God allows for human frailty, I can now accept it in myself and in others. I can allow the memory of a mother who might not want to discuss something that she considered private. She had a diplomatic yet kind way of shutting the door to conversation when she felt it was needed, and shut it remained. I can be frustrated about conversations like that. I wish I'd compelled her to talk more intimately with me.

I believe that misconceptions about God stem from a problem that plagues the whole church, and it is rooted in childhood with our first introduction to God. We believe in the unconditional love of God when it comes to salvation, but we believe we must perform our own daily living. Perhaps we are obedient out of guilt. We hear too many pastors say, "You ought to do this. You owe it to God after all He's done for you." If only we could remember that serving God is a choice that is made out of grateful response to His love for us. How tragic when one serves out of impersonal obligation. His work becomes law, not life.

It was challenging to work through all of this. A lifetime of ingrained thinking does not disappear with the first flash of insight. It takes work, the courage to stand and face the past, to kick open the doors and deal with what one finds.

I'll never forget the day I wrote to my counselor to inform him that I had finally found the answer to one of the most nagging questions that had come out of our last visit together. The question was, "How can God love me if He expects me to spend my entire life becoming more like Him?" I wrote, "It dawned on me several days ago that I am not to become someone else. I was created in God's image. It is the fall of man that marred it. The rest of life is a restoration process to become the person He created. It is not only to become more like Christ; it is also to become more like the me God originally intended. God already sees me as perfect in His Son's image."

The counselor was right in his prediction. Things did get worse before they got better. Introspection revealed my personal inadequacies and misperceptions. But his prediction gave me a road map. My pain was no longer the eternal, unending, despairing type. I knew I was involved in a process that had limits and parameters, and I was determined to work through them slowly, believing that the rewards would be great.

Time for the Audience Reaction

Once the song writing and recording process is complete, the message can then begin to have impact. The solitude the studio offered was a necessity, but its purpose has now been fulfilled. The song is born—its life begun.

And so the crafting of our life's statement is eventually finished. The exhilaration of the mountain-top experiences is enhanced and contrasted by the fine-tuning that occurs during the introspection while in the valley.

The heavenly Father oversees all, knowing the end will bring the rewards of true security. For the pathway into His arms elates the souls of those who are willing to pursue the process.

And those watching from near or afar can truly be encouraged to join in the journey when the lyrics being sung by the traveler reveal the reflections of God's all-encompassing love.

15

In retrospect, God has gifted me with time to recognize and accept my limitations, guiding me in new discoveries about Himself. Good days are now plentiful. I feel the journey toward wholeness and spiritual health has been and continues to be worth the necessary effort. There is a sense of fulfillment in knowing that you have clung tightly to God's hand and found the courage to stare life in the face. Although it is much more comfortable to write the song of our lives with only the range of experiences that reflect the peaks—those exhilarating moments of joy—how monotonous the lyrics become without the contrast of time spent in the valley.

Are you now standing at a crossroad trying to decide which way to go? Either path will expose you to pain. Whether it's infertility, bereavement, or depression, none of us is exempt from the obstacles and unexpected detours that life brings.

One of the paths offers the least resistance. It encourages one to run from pain and pretend that the detours don't hurt much. However, the final destination promises little more than shallow living. The other road asks one to take an honest look along the way. Fears are to be faced, disappointments are to be felt, and losses are to be mourned. The way is thorny, but the one traveling this path is eligible to know the joy that comes from holding onto God for dear life. He will then be able to successfully support friends who stumble alongside him.

The first part of the journey requires time to rest and reflect, sheltered in the promise that he is unconditionally loved by God. This is necessary if he is to find the strength God offers, allowing him then to work his way through other barriers.

Personally, much of my struggle was ended when I could finally accept that I am cherished by a loving God. God's love was reinforced, and I came to grips with the assurance that it is totally unconditional. I began to enjoy the essence of faith. I can't make Him love me any more or any less than He already does.

Life for a person constantly working for God's approval is joyless. It may not be evident when life is going great, for when we function on an even keel, serving the King requires little faith. But when problems come, we can only muster up so much resolve to perform for God. Instead of finding Christ to be of support, we perceive Him as a taskmaster, withholding His praise and approval until we jump through the right hoops. We think He expects a perfect performance. It is this distorted picture, I am convinced, that causes some to desert God when under trial. When this abandonment of faith occurs, it may indicate that the life was lived void of a vital relationship with Christ, built instead on lists of rules and behavioral choices.

Realizing that God cherishes us will change the dimension of our suffering. And if our pain is caused by the failure of an earthly relationship, the healing is even more significant. When we are assured of our place in His heart, we are free to taste fully of the many stages of pain, realizing that God is patient with us while we work our way through grief, anger, depression, and even doubts about Him.

Am I saying the hurt is all gone? No. It remains painful to probe a tender spot and realize that there's more room for growth. I frequently need to remind myself that God is big enough to handle my humanness.

Perhaps you have started down the road of denial. Some live and die in it, having breezed through life in some shallow form, thereby being robbed of the joy of discovering a God who is sufficient. Be willing to face the shadows. Admit life hurts, and deal with it. Stop pretending that you are taking everything in stride, for only then will you see the truth. The truth is this: When we are free to be ourselves with our heavenly Father, He can then tenderly take care of us. He has told us that things will work together for good if we love Him. That love is exhibited when we respect Him enough to entrust ourselves to His care. Cradled in His arms, we can find the joy that sustains us through all of life's experiences.

Today when I speak in concerts and tell my story, I watch people's expressions and their body language to see how many will identify with what I'm talking about. I say, "Maybe you've come tonight, having recently sat at a kitchen table like I did, overwhelmed with life, not having the energy to lift a coffee cup and take a sip."

It's amazing how many drop their eyes to the floor and look back at me a moment later with tears of admission. Is that where you are? I make no claims that you can be on top again in no time and with no effort. God gives you a hope that offers a life preserver that can pull you from the edge of despair.

I value the time after each concert that I'm able to step down from the stage and stand next to those who give me the privilege of hearing the lyrics of both joy and sadness that make up the song of their lives. Would you honor me by sharing the same? Although a personal response to every letter is not always possible, I value the opportunity to grow by being your audience. Your letter will reach me by writing:

Christine
Box 8
Loveland, OH 45140

I can envision pouring a fresh cup of coffee at my kitchen table, propping my feet up, and giving your heart a hug as I read your letter.

Perhaps you've come to this book searching for some basic answers about your relationship with God. Have you ever been introduced to the living Christ? Only a relationship with Him can offer true security—both now and for all eternity. It would be our delight to see you become fully alive by showing God's plan for you to enjoy eternal life.

Today, as I conclude writing this chapter, the last of the blueberries my mother picked have finally found their way from the freezer into a batch of muffins and are baking in the oven. The aroma soothes the loss and brings sweet memories.

And life goes on. Ron was a bit discouraged this morning over a problem at work. Jaime seems to be struggling with her best friend at school, and I have to deal this afternoon with an acquaintance who is considering suicide.

Producing the song of our lives is much harder and unappealing at times than producing an actual song like "Carry Me." The studio can be a welcome escape. It is a musician's utopia, for in it I am transported to another world. The instruments play perfectly in my ears, and my voice is adjusted until it's pleasing. Producing one's life's song, however, is infinitely more challenging and rewarding.

Oh, I'll go to Nashville again and sing my song, but just now I want to stay here and live it.